N.   Tentes servantes d'offices
O.   Maison du Boucher chargé du soin de la basse cour.
P.   Les forges, l'armurier, & le Coutelier
Q.   Le four
R.   Baraque de l'apothicaire et des garçons Chirurgiens
S.   hopital

T.   Chaloupe sur le Chantier de 22. p.ds de Quille & de 5.ds soliveau
     7.p.s & 9.p.s de bau & de 2.p.s 4 p.s de franc
V.   Batean servant à descharger les chaloupes qui viennent à la rade
X.   Rigoles à planter pour faire une jettée
Y.   Sentine de ces bateaux que l'on vuar chercher du vieil bibois
     Mon.r le Directeur de la Compagnie

Eighteenth-Century Florida

and Its Borderlands

Eighteenth-Century Florida

and Its Borderlands

Edited by
SAMUEL PROCTOR

A University of Florida Book

The University Presses of Florida

Gainesville / 1975

Papers read at the First Annual Bicentennial Symposium sponsored by the American Revolution Bicentennial Commission of Florida, held at the University of Florida, May 18–20, 1972

Library of Congress Cataloging in Publication Data
Main entry under title:

Eighteenth-century Florida and its borderlands.

"A University of Florida book."
"Papers read at the first annual Bicentennial symposium sponsored by the American Revolution Bicentennial Commission of Florida, held at the University of Florida, May 18–20, 1972."
    1. Florida—History—To 1821—Congresses.
I. Proctor, Samuel, ed. II. American Revolution Bicentennial Commission of Florida.
F314.E34   975.9'02   74–31385
ISBN 0–8130–0408–X

PRINTED BY THE STORTER PRINTING COMPANY, INCORPORATED
GAINESVILLE, FLORIDA

Introduction

SAMUEL PROCTOR

THERE was much consternation in England when it was learned that His Majesty's peace commissioners in Paris had agreed in 1762 to accept Florida as the price for the return of Havana to Spain. Pitt, in his great speech on the preliminaries of peace, delivered in the House of Commons on December 9, 1762, condemned this "most atrocious bargain." Havana was the key to the great treasures and riches of Spain in America. A sketch in *Gentleman's Magazine* described Florida as "pine barrens, or sandy desarts [*sic*]." One writer sarcastically claimed that the area would be useful only as a supplier of peat for the island of Jamaica. Some looked more kindly on the arrangement, however. Since Florida was in the same latitude as Persia, it was expected that it might produce similar commodities such as silk. General Jeffrey Amherst, British commander-in-chief in America, supported the acquisition; it would round out his command on the continent of North America, from the Florida Keys north into Canada. Amherst argued the advantages of St. Augustine as a base for operations against the French in time of war, and he called for a "Capital Settlement" there.

The fact is that few in Britain knew much about Florida. For the next two decades the British remained in Florida before retroceding the territory to Spain in 1783. Physical remains of the British period are few. Most of its population emigrated, abandoning farms and plantations. Soon these properties were overgrown and hard to discover. The British period in Florida became almost a forgotten episode, and scholars have continued to neglect this era. While Florida never became a major theater of military operations during the American Revolution, it did play an important role in America during the eighteenth century. Many important people lived in Florida, and events occurring elsewhere in America and in Europe had a major impact there. Florida's role before and during the American revolution has never been fully recounted. This is now a primary responsibility for scholars and researchers.

The Florida Bicentennial Commission was created by the state legislature in 1970, effective July 4 of that year, to plan and develop Florida's participation in the celebration of the two hundredth anniversary of the American Revolution. One of the important goals of the Bicentennial, nationally and in Florida, is to recall our heritage and to place it in its proper historical perspective. In order to re-examine our origins, our historic values, and the role that Florida has played in the nation, the Florida Bicentennial Commission appointed a committee on publications and research. Its plans are to publish twenty-five facsimiles of rare, out-of-print books on Florida history, a series of school pamphlets, and several specialized monographs, including a history of the Revolutionary period in Florida. A series of five symposia was planned, to be held annually, beginning in 1972 and continuing through the Bicentennial year. The state university campuses were designated as the meeting places for these conferences, and distinguished scholars were invited to participate. The plan was to investigate in depth various aspects of the political, economic, intellectual, and social events of eighteenth-century Florida, and to make this information available, not only at the conferences but in published form. Toward that goal the Florida Bicentennial Commission has authorized the publication by the University Presses of Florida of this first volume, *Eighteenth-Century Florida and Its Borderlands.* Four other volumes will follow.

"Eighteenth-Century Florida and Its Borderlands" was selected as the first theme to be examined critically. The two Florida colonies, as they were designated in the Proclamation of October 7, 1763, became part of Britain's far-flung American empire after the Seven Years' War, or the French and Indian War as it is known in American history. A peaceful land, peopled by settlers drawn from abroad and from the northern colonies, was the major goal of the English government. Florida industry, agriculture, and trade would be encouraged, and the inhabitants of these new southern colonies were promised the benefits of the laws of England. The people of East and West Florida could not and did not live isolated from the rest of America and the world. The colonies related especially to their borderlands—Georgia and the Carolinas to the north, Louisiana to the west, and the Caribbean to the south. The politics, the economics, the way of life in these areas affected the people of Florida—whites, blacks, and Indians. The purpose of the First Bicentennial Symposium was the examination by competent scholars of some of the internal and external problems that eighteenth-century Floridians faced.

The symposium was held at the University of Florida, Gainesville, May 18–20, 1972. Thomas W. Cole, Sr., welcomed the participants to the campus. Representing the Florida Bicentennial Commission was Pat Dodson of Pensacola, its vice chairman. John K. Mahon, professor of history, University of Florida, Michael V. Gannon, professor of history and religion, University of Florida, and Carl Feiss, director, Urban and Regional Development Center, University of Florida, served as chairmen for the three program sessions.

Special thanks are owed to many people whose help made the symposium and its related activities a success. These include N. E. (Bill) Miller, then executive director of the Florida Bicentennial Commission, and Rosemary Mason of the commission staff, Tallahassee; Roy C. Craven, Jr., director of The Gallery, University of Florida, for the Larry Rivers Exhibition and a reception in The Gallery; Luis Arana of the Castillo de San Marcos, St. Augustine, for the tour of that seventeenth-century Spanish fortification and a demonstration of its military weaponry; the Historic St. Augustine Restoration Board for the tour of the restored area; and Carver Harris and the members and officers of the St. Augustine Historical Society for the reception in the gardens of The Oldest House.

The University of Florida faculty committee on arrangements included Roy C. Craven, Jr., The Gallery; John K. Mahon, Department of History; F. Blair Reeves, Department of Architecture; Claude C. Sturgill, Department of History; Eldon R. Turner, Department of History; and Samuel Proctor, Department of History, chairman. B. R. Blair, coordinator, Department of Special Programs, administered the symposium.

Symposium Participants

JOHN J. TEPASKE, a graduate of Michigan State University and Duke University, is professor of history at Duke University. A recipient of a Ford Foundation Fellowship at the University of California, Berkeley, 1962–63, he has served as visiting professor at the University of Washington and the University of Texas. He is the author of *The Governorship of Spanish Florida* and the editor of *Three American Empires, The Character of Philip II: The Problem of Moral Judgements in History,* and *Explosive Forces in Latin America.* His articles have appeared in scholarly and professional journals in the United States and Mexico.

HELEN HORNBECK TANNER has been engaged in ethnohistorical research on the Caddo Tribe of Oklahoma under a federal contract through the Bureau of Indian Affairs. She has prepared reports and appeared as expert witness before the Indian Claims Commission since 1962, and was a member of the Commission on Indian Affairs, State of Michigan, from 1966 to 1970. She is the author of *Zéspedes in East Florida, 1784–1790, General Green Visits Saint Augustine,* and *Opportunities for Women through Education,* in addition to being a frequent contributor to the *Florida Historical Quarterly* and other scholarly journals. Dr. Tanner holds her graduate degrees from the University of Florida and the University of Michigan.

WILLIAM C. STURTEVANT is curator of North American Anthropology at the Smithsonian Institution. He holds a doctorate from Yale University, where his thesis topic was "The Mikasuki Seminole: Medical Beliefs and Practices." He has done extensive research in ethnohistory of the Indians of eastern North America. He served at Yale University as a research associate and instructor in the anthropology department, and was also assistant curator of anthropology at the Peabody Museum at Yale University. Dr. Sturtevant was the recipient of a Fulbright Award and has lectured at the Institute of Social Anthropology, Oxford University.

MICHAEL G. KAMMEN, professor of history at Cornell University, was winner in 1973 of the Pulitzer Prize for history for his book *People of Paradox: An Inquiry Concerning the Origins of American Civilization*. He has been an instructor of history at Harvard University and has received the National Endowment for Humanities Fellowship. Besides his Pulitzer Prize–winning book, Professor Kammen is the author of seven other volumes, including *Hope of Sand: The Colonial Agents, British Politics, and the American Revolution*, and *Politics and Society in Colonial America*. His degrees are from George Washington University and Harvard University.

ROBERT R. REA, a graduate of Friends University and Indiana University, is a native of Kansas. He has been Research Professor of History and is Alumni Professor and Graduate Study Chairman in the Department of History, Auburn University. He has also served as visiting professor at Indiana University and the University of Virginia. As an English historian with trans-Atlantic interests, he has published *The English Press in Politics 1760–1774*, *The Memoire Justificatif of the Chevalier Montault de Monberaut: Indian Diplomacy in British West Florida, 1763–1765* (with Milo B. Howard), and has contributed to the *Florida Historical Quarterly*, *Louisiana History*, *Alabama Review*, *Indiana Magazine of History*, and other professional and scholarly journals.

LOUIS DE VORSEY, JR., was for seven years head of the Department of Geography, University of Georgia. A major area of his scholarly interest is historical geography. He is author of *De Brahm's Report of the General Survey in the Southern District of North America* and *The Indian Boundary in the Southern Colonies, 1763–1775*, co-author of several textbooks, and a frequent contributor of articles and reviews to scholarly publications. He has lectured at the University of Liverpool, University College, London, and the Institute of Historical Research, London. He was awarded an Association of American Geographers research grant and a National Science Foundation grant in support of his doctoral research. Professor De Vorsey's graduate degrees are from Indiana University and the University of London.

PAUL H. SMITH was a member of the history faculty at Memphis State University and the University of Florida and served as chairman of the Department of History, University of Nevada. He is a graduate of Bowling Green State University and the University of Michigan. Since 1969 he has been director of the Library of Congress' American Revolution Bicentennial staff. He is the author of *Loyalists and Redcoats* and the editor of *English Defenders of American Freedoms,* a volume of American Revolutionary pamphlets. He is joint author of a guide to American Revolutionary manuscripts in the Library of Congress, and he is presently editing the multivolume edition of *Letters of Delegates to Congress, 1774–1789.*

SAMUEL WILSON, JR., is a prominent New Orleans architect and a member of the faculty of Tulane University, where he lectures on the historical architecture of Louisiana. He received the Edward Langley Scholarship from the American Institute of Architects in 1938 to study and travel in Europe, where he did research on the origins of Louisiana architecture in France. He is a recognized authority on the architecture of Louisiana and the Gulf coast. He is an Elected Fellow, American Institute of Architects, and has served as vice-president and board member of the New Orleans chapter of the institute. He is a native of New Orleans and is a graduate of Tulane University.

JESSIE J. POESCH, a native of Iowa, is professor of art history at Newcomb College, Tulane University. Her awards have included grants from the American Philosophical Society and the National Endowment for the Humanities. She is author of one book and several scholarly articles, and was compiler of the catalogue *The Early Furniture of Louisiana* for a major exhibition at the Louisiana State Museum in 1972. Professor Poesch was also curatorial assistant at the Henry Francis du Pont Winterthur Museum.

CHARLES VAN RAVENSWAAY is director of the Henry Francis du Pont Winterthur Museum, Winterthur, Delaware, and a member of the executive committee of the National Trust for Historic Preservation. His major interests are architectural history and American arts and history. He is editor and co-author of *Missouri—A Guide to the "Show Me" State* and a number of articles. A graduate of Washington University, he has received an honorary degree from Maryville College of the Sacred Heart and serves on a number of national and international boards and committees.

Contents

The Fugitive Slave: Intercolonial Rivalry and Spanish Slave
   Policy, 1687–1764 / John J. TePaske / 1

Pipesmoke and Muskets: Florida Indian Intrigues of the
   Revolutionary Era / Helen Hornbeck Tanner / 13

Commentary / William C. Sturtevant / 40

The Unique and the Universal in the History of New World
   Colonization / Michael G. Kammen / 48

British West Florida: Stepchild of Diplomacy / Robert R. Rea / 61

De Brahm's East Florida on the Eve of Revolution: The Materials
   for Its Re-creation / Louis De Vorsey, Jr. / 78

Commentary / Paul H. Smith / 97

Architecture in Eighteenth-Century West Florida / Samuel
   Wilson, Jr. / 102

Colonial Painting and Furniture in a Florida Borderland / Jessie
   J. Poesch / 140

Commentary / Charles van Ravenswaay / 154

The Fugitive Slave: Intercolonial Rivalry and Spanish Slave Policy, 1687–1764

JOHN J. TEPASKE

BEFORE 1670, intercolonial conflicts in the colonial Southeast were rare. Although England battled Spain in the Caribbean and on the Isthmus of Panama in the early and mid-seventeenth century, Spaniards in Florida and Englishmen in settlements dotting the eastern seaboard remained isolated and insulated from one another. But the founding of Carolina in 1670 shattered the tranquility of the English-Spanish frontier. Carolinians and Floridians began contesting bitterly for the friendship and allegiance of the Indians; border clashes broke out over unsettled territory; bands of English Indians ravaged Spanish missions; and Spanish Indians took reprisals on newly established British settlements.[1] Another issue which heightened tension was the fugitive slave problem, significant not only to the international rivalry in the Southeast but also to the development of Spanish and English slave policies.

Slavery never had deep roots in Spanish Florida. Some blacks accompanied Pedro Menéndez de Avilés in 1565, but only a few entered the struggling colony during the last half of the century. In 1602, royal treasury officials listed fifty-six blacks—thirty-six old slaves and twenty new ones.[2] For 1604, a modern authority reports only thirty-four Negroes—eighteen able-bodied men, nine women, and seven too old to work.[3] Primarily a military outpost, Florida

1. See particularly Verner W. Crane, *The Southern Frontier, 1670–1732* (Durham, N.C., 1928).
2. Charles W. Arnade, *Florida on Trial, 1593–1602* (Miami, 1959), pp. 8–9.
3. John R. Dunkle, "Population Changes as an Element in the Historical Geography of St. Augustine," *Florida Historical Quarterly* 37 (July 1958):5.

had no need for slave labor. Indians, criminals, and forced laborers from New Spain and Cuba worked on the colony's fortifications.

At the beginning of the eighteenth century, the number of blacks slowly began to increase; Negro militiamen arrived from Cuba to defend St. Augustine and a few fugitive slaves came from Carolina. By 1746, almost a third of the population of St. Augustine was black, 403 out of 1,509.[4] As the frontier became more secure after the War of Jenkins' Ear, this number tended to remain static: Florida's population grew to over 3,000 inhabitants by the end of the First Spanish Period, but there were only 429 blacks and mulattoes in the colony at the time of its evacuation in 1764.[5]

The rapid growth of the slave population in South Carolina during the same period provides a sharp contrast to Florida's pattern. With the development of rice production in the 1690s, large numbers of blacks entered the colony and soon outnumbered whites. Although contemporary accounts are not completely reliable, they do provide some indication of how slavery took hold. In 1703, whites outnumbered blacks 4,220 to 3,250, but by 1708 they were virtually even at 4,100 blacks and 4,080 whites. By 1715, there were 10,500 Negroes to 6,250 whites; in 1721, it was 11,800 to 7,800; and by 1740, the gap had widened—39,000 to 20,000. In 1763, approximately 90,000 blacks toiled in South Carolina, twice the number of whites and almost thirty times the total population of Florida at that time.[6]

Although Carolinians were reluctant to pass laws defining a slave's legal status, they were quick to lay down laws controlling his conduct. As the black population grew, these regulations were rigorously enforced. Rebellious or runaway slaves faced severe punishments—whipping, branding, nose slitting, and emasculation. Even so, slave rebellions broke out periodically in the first seventy years of colonial development—in 1711, 1714, and three times in 1739. In 1740, a new slave code and a more rigorous system for control of the black population prevented the outbreak of new revolts.[7] But rebellions were not the only way for slaves to protest their lot in Carolina—some attempted to escape to Spanish St. Augustine.

4. Ibid., p. 7.
5. Robert L. Gold, *Borderland Empires in Transition: The Triple-Nation Transfer of Florida* (Carbondale and Edwardsville, Ill., 1969), p. 76.
6. M. Eugene Sirmans, *Colonial South Carolina: A Political History, 1663–1763* (Chapel Hill, N.C., 1966), pp. 60, 107, 132, 207, 347.
7. Ibid., pp. 64–66.

The first fugitive slaves reached the Florida capital in September 1687, asking for sanctuary and for instruction in the Roman Catholic faith. Unsure of what course to follow, Governor Diego de Quiroga y Losada put the eight men to work on the Castillo de San Marcos, assigned the two women to his residence as servants, appointed a priest to teach the group catechism, and sought instructions from Spain regarding their disposition. When an English agent appeared in St. Augustine a short time later, demanding their return, Quiroga refused. The slaves had proved willing workers, had embraced Roman Catholicism, and had legally married. All were terrified of being returned to their English masters. Explaining to the English agent that he was powerless to act without orders from Spain, Quiroga offered to purchase the ten slaves for 160 pesos each, payable in eighteen months because he had no funds available in his treasury. The Carolinian accepted the proposal and agreed to return in a year and a half for the 1,600 pesos.[8] Quiroga solicited the money from New Spain, but when it arrived he immediately diverted it to his soldiers for salaries and rations. When the English agent returned to collect, Quiroga's money was gone. All he received from Quiroga was a promise to pay at the earliest possible moment, but there is no evidence he ever received anything for the ten runaways.[9]

Although Governor Quiroga had kept the Negroes in St. Augustine, their status as slaves or freedmen was still not clear. Did conversion to Roman Catholicism make them eligible for emancipation? On November 7, 1693, a royal *cédula* (order-in-council) resolved the issue by granting the ten Negroes a kind of semi-emancipation. By adopting the Roman Catholic religion they received legal status as free men, but they could not leave Florida and they were ordered to continue work on the fortifications at St. Augustine. Their condition closely resembled that of a medieval serf.[10] The royal cédula of November 7 was the first step in defining a fugitive slave policy: runaways coming into Florida from Carolina could obtain

8. AGI (Archivo General de Indias), Santo Domingo (Audiencia of Santo Domingo), 54–5–12. Los oficiales reales de la Florida al rey, March 8, 1689, in *Journal of Negro History* 9 (April 1924):151–52.

9. AGI, Santo Domingo, 54–5–12. Carta del gobernador de la Florida al rey, June 8, 1690. Carta de los oficiales reales de la Florida al rey, May 20, 1690, in *Journal of Negro History* 9 (April 1924):154–64.

10. Cited in AGI, Santo Domingo, Legajo 842. Carta del gobernador de la Florida al rey, November 2, 1725.

their freedom if they embraced the Catholic faith, but in other ways they were sharply restricted.

The new slave policy neither stimulated a large influx of fugitive slaves into Florida nor did it cause a stir in Carolina. Although a few blacks may have risked the dangers of the trek to St. Augustine, there is no evidence of any successful flights into Florida until 1725. Three slaves made the attempt in 1697, but were caught and emasculated; one of the three died from his punishment.[11] Such examples helped to inhibit the flight of the blacks, but also important were the Indian allies which the Carolinians had gained during Queen Anne's War. Creeks, Yamasees, Cherokees, and Catawbas served the English as slave catchers and were given a free hand with reprisals on any luckless runaways they caught.[12]

The fugitive slave problem arose again in the spring of 1725. Seven fugitives from Carolina entered St. Augustine, asking for refuge and conversion to Roman Catholicism. Reluctant to take action without orders from Spain, Governor Antonio de Benavides followed the example of Quiroga. He put the seven blacks to work at Fort San Marcos, began their instruction in the Catholic religion, wrote to Madrid for further orders, and sent Cavalry Captain Joseph Primo de Rivera and Accountant Francisco Menéndez Marqués to Charleston with instructions to offer Governor Francis Nicholson 200 pesos each for the seven runaways.[13] The two agents got a cold reception from Nicholson and his council. Nicholson claimed that the slaves were worth far more than the amount suggested and that he would be content with nothing less than their immediate return. Truculent and abusive, the Carolina governor intimated that war might result if Benavides did not acquiesce to his demands. When the two agents finally returned to St. Augustine, the Florida governor refused to be intimidated. He kept the seven slaves in Florida and awaited instructions from Spain.[14]

In Madrid, the Council of the Indies faced a real dilemma: it had discovered two precedents for setting a policy of runaway slaves, but they were contradictory. In 1693, Charles II had freed the ten

11. Sirmans, *Colonial South Carolina*, p. 66.
12. Crane, *Southern Frontier*, pp. 71–107.
13. Actually Primo de Rivera and Menéndez Marqués entered Charleston with instructions to report on the military situation there and to protest the building of Fort King George on the banks of the Altamaha.
14. AGI, Santo Domingo, Legajo 842. Carta del gobernador de la Florida al rey, November 2, 1725.

runaway blacks from Carolina who had become Roman Catholic, but his example was not followed later. In the first two decades of the eighteenth century an increasing number of blacks had escaped French Haiti to seek refuge in Spanish Española. When the French ambassador at Madrid pressed for return of the fugitives in 1722, the council ordered that all those who could be rounded up easily be restored to their owners in Haiti. To ferret out and return those who had fled to the mountains would be too costly, but return of the other runaways would restore good relations with the French.[15]

To resolve the dilemma the council sought the opinion of its *fiscal* (solicitor or crown attorney). In January 1727, the fiscal argued that the precedent of 1693 ruled in the current case of the seven fugitive slaves. If the ten original runaways had been given their freedom because they had adopted Roman Catholicism, the seven recent arrivals in St. Augustine should be governed by the same policy. The fiscal also recommended that the financial burden of paying off their English owners should be assumed by the slaves themselves who could work off the purchase price. Usually the council concurred in the fiscal's decision, but two contingencies proved strong enough to override him—the price to be paid their English masters and the status of the slaves who refused to accept Roman Catholicism. The council was not sure that the Florida treasury could or should bear the burden of payment, and humanitarianism dictated that no slave should be restored to his English owner—and certain death—if he refused to accept the faith.[16] Nothing was decided.

Benavides grew increasingly apprehensive about the possibility of war over the seven runaways and repeatedly pressed his superiors for a decision. In 1729, another fiscal drew up a brief for consideration by the Council of the Indies. Using the same arguments as those presented two years earlier, the fiscal agreed that the return of fugitive slaves to Haiti from Española had restored good relations with the French, but that runaways coming into Florida from Carolina fit a different pattern. They sought refuge in St. Augustine because of a desire to become Roman Catholic; this passion for conversion was the vital factor which should insure their emancipation and retention in Florida. This time the council agreed with the fiscal but urged Benavides to offer no more than a just price for the

15. AGI, Santo Domingo, Legajo 2530. Consulta del Consejo de las Indias, April 12, 1731.
16. Ibid.

Negroes, giving due thought to their age, ambition, and robustness.[17] This had already been taken care of—Benavides and the principal military leaders of the colony had voted to pay 200 pesos for each slave.[18]

Four years later, Philip V confirmed the decision of the Council of the Indies but with modifications. In cédulas of October 4 and October 29, 1733, he granted freedom to all runaways who adopted Roman Catholicism and served a four-year term as public or state slaves in St. Augustine. He ordered that there be no compensation to their former owners, since the English never paid for Spanish slaves who fled to British dominions. The Spanish king hoped that the new policy would stimulate the mass exodus of slaves from Carolina, thereby disrupting the economy and severely weakening the colony, which had been illegally usurped from Spain.[19] In 1738, Governor Manuel de Montiano began putting this policy into effect; he freed the fifty or more fugitives who had recently come into St. Augustine and requested that the governor of Cuba return those runaways who had been sold to Spaniards on the island.[20] Two years later Philip V further defined fugitive slave policy in Florida. He freed all those who promised to become Roman Catholic and lifted the four-year labor requirement.[21] Ten years later, in 1750, Ferdinand VI extended the policy to all provinces of New Spain.[22]

The threat of English invasion, first from Carolina and then from Georgia, gave a new role to blacks in the beleaguered Florida colony. In the seventeenth century they had served as laborers and servants; in the eighteenth century they were incorporated into the militia as defenders of St. Augustine against enemy attacks. Negroes first rose to prominence in military ranks in 1728 during Colonel

17. Ibid.

18. AGI, Santo Domingo, Legajo 844. Auto y demas diligencias sobre los negros de la Florida, January 1730.

19. AGI, Santo Domingo, 58-1-31. Carta del gobernador de la Florida al rey, May 31, 1738, in *Journal of Negro History* 9 (April 1924):173-74. Montiano cites the cédulas in this letter.

20. AGI, Santo Domingo, 58-1-31. Carta del gobernador de la Florida al rey, February 16, 1739, in *Journal of Negro History* 9 (April 1924):176-78.

21. AGI, Santo Domingo, Legajo 838. Real cédula, San Lorenzo, November 11, 1740; Consulta del Consejo de las Indias, March 11, 1740.

22. AGI, Santo Domingo, 58-1-33. Carta del gobernador de la Florida al rey, September 10, 1751, in *Journal of Negro History* 9 (April 1924): 183. This document acknowledges receipt of the royal decree.

John Palmer's raid on St. Augustine. They served so valiantly in defense of the town that Benavides freed all those who took arms against the English. As a tribute to their efforts, he did away with the St. Augustine slave market.[23] Extolling the virtues of black soldiers to the Council of the Indies, the governor suggested that the Spanish use freed blacks from Carolina to foment rebellion among the 15,000 slaves there. He advocated paying the blacks for English scalps as the English paid Indians for Spanish scalps. Having seen them at their best during Palmer's raid, he was now anxious to use blacks as military pawns in his struggle against the English. Negroes, it appeared, were more reliable allies than the Indians.[24]

As more fugitive slaves began trickling into St. Augustine in the late 1730s, Governor Manuel de Montiano took another step in defining Spanish fugitive slave policy in Florida. Sometime in the spring of 1738—the exact date is not clear—he established a new village for freed runaways, one-half league north of St. Augustine; it was called Gracia Real Santa Teresa de Mosa. Thirty-eight recent fugitive slaves became the nucleus of the new settlement. In November 1738, twenty-three additional runaways arrived to join the tiny village. Montiano wrote that he found it "efficacious to have them segregated."[25]

From what little is known of the first fort at Mosa, "it was four square with a flanker at each corner, banked round with earth," and surrounded by a moat lined with yucca. Inside the fort were a lookout, some houses, and a well.[26] Hoping that the Negroes would begin farming and eventually provide food for the people of St. Augustine, Montiano appointed Sebastián Sánchez to assist the new settlement. To instruct the blacks in the Roman Catholic faith, he named the student priest Joseph de León. Montiano began organizing a detachment of black militia for use in the future defense of

23. AGI, Santo Domingo, Legajo 833. Consulta del Consejo de las Indias, April 27, 1733.
24. Ibid.
25. AGI, Santo Domingo, Legajo 844. Carta del gobernador de la Florida al rey, June 10, 1738; Carta del gobernador de la Florida al rey, February 16, 1739.
26. For descriptions of Mosa, I am endebted to Mr. Luis Arana of the Castillo de San Marcos National Monument, St. Augustine; he provided me with an unpublished paper on Mosa. See *The St. Augustine Expedition of 1740. A Report to the South Carolina General Assembly* (Columbia, S.C., 1954), p. 25.

Florida.[27] The blacks themselves informed Philip V that they were the "bitterest enemies of the English" and promised to shed "their last drop of blood in defense of Spain and the Holy Faith."[28]

The establishment of Mosa had severe repercussions in Carolina and Georgia. In February 1739, the Governor of Georgia, James Oglethorpe, wrote that slaves in Carolina leaned toward "liberty and revolt." Spanish offers of freedom had fostered rebelliousness among English slaves, and they would soon rise in revolt.[29] In Florida, Montiano boasted to Philip V that the new town of Mosa and the emancipation program had increased unrest among the slaves in Carolina.[30] These were not idle statements. In September 1739, slaves near Charleston seized a cache of arms and marched through the countryside, burning several plantations and killing twenty-one whites. The capture and immediate execution of forty-four insurgent blacks and the bloody reprisals by bands of Chickasaw and Catawba Indians helped quell the revolt, but not until the angry slaves had panicked many white inhabitants. Governor William Bull blamed the revolt on Montiano's fugitive slave policy.[31]

The new village of Mosa did not last long. Increased hostilities along the frontier and the outbreak of the War of Jenkins' Ear forced its evacuation—all the blacks were moved into St. Augustine.[32] When Oglethorpe swept into Florida in May 1740, freed blacks again rallied to the side of their Spanish benefactors. Twenty black soldiers participated in Captain Antonio Salgado's assault on Colonel John Palmer's troops at Mosa on June 25–26, a Spanish victory that was crucial in lifting Oglethorpe's siege.[33]

Montiano apparently had the full support of the fugitive slaves,

27. East Florida Papers, Washington, 37–113. Carta del gobernador de la Florida al gobernador de Cuba, January 3, 1739, 136v–137v. Cited in the unpublished paper by Luis Arana.

28. AGI, Santo Domingo, 58–1–31. Un pliego de los Negroes Fugitivos de los Plantages de Yngleses á S. M., June 10, 1738, in Journal of Negro History 9 (April 1924):175.

29. Colonial Office, London (hereafter CO), 5:654, pt. 1. James Oglethorpe to the Duke of Newcastle, St. Simons, February 23, 1739.

30. AGI, Santo Domingo, Legajo 2584. Carta del gobernador de la Florida al rey, August 16, 1739.

31. CO 5:384. Copy of a letter from Governor William Bull to the Lord Commissioners of Trade and Plantations, Charles Town, October 5, 1739.

32. AGI, Santo Domingo, 58–1–32. Carta del gobernador de la Florida al rey, September 25, 1740, in Journal of Negro History 9 (April 1924):182.

33. AGI, Santo Domingo, Legajo 845. Carta del gobernador de la Florida al rey, August 9, 1740.

but one English observer believed otherwise. In 1741, Kenneth Baily reported to his superiors in London that the Florida governor had not kept his word in granting freedom to fugitive slaves and had kept them at hard labor on the fortifications at St. Augustine. He argued that these blacks were so dissatisfied that they would refuse to fight on the Spanish side if the English attacked Florida again.[34] Evidently this rumor was unfounded. In July 1742, at least 500 black troops, many from Cuba, joined Montiano in his abortive attempt to take Frederica.[35]

Sometime after the close of the War of Jenkins' Ear—probably in 1748—Mosa was re-established, both as a refuge for the blacks and as a northern defense post for St. Augustine proper. To drill the inhabitants and direct their agricultural and building pursuits, Governor Melchor de Navarrete placed an infantry captain and a lieutenant in the settlement; for their religious instruction he appointed the Franciscan Andres de Vilches. With funds that had been allocated for the Indians, the royal warehouse in St. Augustine provided essential food and supplies to the village.[36] Navarrete's successor, Interim Governor Fulgencio García de Solís, strengthened the defenses of Mosa by rebuilding the walls, setting up a permanent guard and five Spanish cavalry regulars (an officer and four enlisted men), providing arms and powder for the detachment of free blacks, and laying plans for artillery emplacements.[37] Between 1756 and 1758 Governor Alonso Fernandez de Heredia carried through this proposal by mounting four small cannon, one on each side of the village. He also reorganized the militia detachment with its own officers. His only failure, he believed, was in not making the village self-sufficient and productive.[38] Montiano's earlier vision of Mosa as the granary for St. Augustine was never realized;

34. CO 55:655, pt. 1. Deposition of Kenneth Baily relating to St. Augustine, Florida, Covent Garden, January 19, 1741.
35. John J. TePaske, *The Governorship of Spanish Florida, 1700–1763* (Durham, N.C., 1964), pp. 148–52.
36. AGI, Santo Domingo, Legajo 2541. Carta del gobernador de la Florida al Marqués de Ensenada, April 2, 1752.
37. AGI, Santo Domingo, 58–1–33. Carta del gobernador de la Florida al rey, December 7, 1752, in *Journal of Negro History* 9 (April 1924):189–92.
38. AGI, Santo Domingo, Legajo 2584. Carta del gobernador de la Florida a Don Julián de Arriaga, April 7, 1756. See also AGI, Santo Domingo, Legajo 846. Informe de lo que ocurre sobre la administración del Pueblo de Moza en la Florida formado de los Negroes fugitivos de las colonas Inglesas a fin de que se tome la providencia conveniente, September 15, 1757.

like the rest of the colony, Mosa was dependent upon outside aid.

By the end of the First Spanish Period, 1763, Mosa at least resembled a viable community. It was located about two and one-half miles north of St. Augustine on the bank of a river (Macaris Creek?) and consisted of several thatched huts and a board chapel about thirty feet long and sixteen feet wide. The river side of the village had no defenses; a moat about three feet wide and two feet deep and two small bastions with a 165-foot curtain defended the land side.[39]

Despite its failure to grow significantly or to lure large numbers of fugitive slaves from English colonies, Mosa symbolized Spanish defiance of the English in the Southeast. The small settlement of freed blacks irritated colonial leaders in South Carolina; they believed its existence created unrest among their slaves. In 1749, Governor William Glen complained that Florida lured slaves away from South Carolina with promises of freedom and a better life. Governor Navarrete's answer was evasive: he said that he would gladly ask Ferdinand VI to review Spanish fugitive slave policy, but that as governor he had no power to revoke royal cédulas or to return runaways.[40] This prompted Glen to send Captain Raymond Damare to St. Augustine to demand the immediate restoration of all fugitive slaves to Carolina. Damare argued that slaves should be handled as were English ships which ran aground in Florida waters—returned to their owners. He then threatened "disagreeable consequences" if Navarrete refused to meet his demands, promising to incite Indians against the black settlement at Mosa and bring war to the "very Gates of Saint Augustine."[41] The Florida governor was not moved. He and his successors responded to the English threat by making the fort and village of Mosa more defensible and habitable for the freed black population (which numbered seventy-nine at the time of the evacuation of the colony in 1763–64).[42]

39. This is the description given in the unpublished paper by Luis Arana, confirmed by the plan of Pablo Castelló drawn up in 1763. See Verne E. Chatelain, *The Defenses of Spanish Florida, 1565–1763* (Washington, 1941), map 13.

40. CO 5:385, pt. 1. Extracts of Governor Glen's Answers to Queries from the Board of Trade and Plantations, 1749; Duke of Bedford to the Board of Trade, Whitehall, May 4, 1750.

41. CO 5:385, pt. 1. Copy of Instructions from his Excellency the Governor (William Glen) to Raymond Damare, Esq., May 4, 1750. AGI, Santo Domingo, Legajo 2584. Carta del gobernador de la Florida al rey, February 15, 1750.

42. Gold, *Borderland Empires*, p. 76.

Between 1670 and 1764, the fugitive slave problem was significant in intercolonial relationships in the Southeast. The liberal Spanish manumission policy and the establishment of Mosa as a lure to slaves in South Carolina created severe intercolonial tensions. In fact, the issue of fugitive slaves ranked with the Indian problem and the territorial disputes as factors disrupting stability and peace on the southern frontier. Although few slaves actually escaped to St. Augustine, the problem persisted for slaveowners and for the governor of Carolina who was responsible for the defense and welfare of the colony. Governor William Bull went so far as to blame the slave rebellion of 1739 on Spanish policy, and the prospect that further revolts might be incited by fugitive slaves continued until 1764.

Analysis of the fugitive slave issue provides some insights into Spanish and English slave policies. On the surface it seems that the Spanish were far more benevolent in their treatment of slaves than were the English. Carolinians viewed their slaves as chattel to be exploited for economic ends, as "a Horse or Ox, after he has bought them."[43] Some groups—like the Society for the Propagation of the Gospel in Foreign Parts—attempted to Christianize and educate blacks in South Carolina, but first they had to convince the owners that education and Christianity would not lead to emancipation.[44] The Spaniards appeared more humane, at least in their policy toward fugitive slaves. Slaves were looked upon as moral beings with souls, and so conversion to Catholicism became an overweening factor in the emancipation of runaways. Once they had adopted the Spanish state religion, they could take their places alongside the Spaniards as free men, at least legally. Actually very few fugitive slaves benefited from the humane laws laid down for their welfare. At the time of the evacuation of Florida in 1764, there were 429 blacks and mulattoes in the colony. Of these, 350 were crown or private slaves; only 79 of them enjoyed free status.[45] One can only conclude that either very few runaways were reaching St. Augustine or that the Spanish preferred to keep the fugitives in slave status.

43. Quoted in Sirmans, *Colonial South Carolina*, p. 66.
44. See Frank J. Klingberg, *An Appraisal of the Negro in Colonial South Carolina: A Study in Americanization* (Washington, 1941). This is a heavily documented study of the work of the SPG among the slaves in South Carolina.
45. Gold, *Borderland Empire*, p. 76.

A second generalization concerns modes of exploitation. In Carolina the English exploited slaves for economic purposes. The black population dominated South Carolina by the mid-eighteenth century and became the basis for the economic development and prosperity of the colony. In Florida fewer blacks were exploited and it was primarily for military and strategic purposes. Having lost out to the English in the competition for Indian allies, the governor in St. Augustine turned to blacks to defend Florida against English incursions and used black militia to wage war against Georgia in 1742. Blacks made able, loyal soldiers—their conduct during Palmer's raid in 1728 and Oglethorpe's siege in 1740 proved that—and the governor was willing to use them for military purposes. He also envisioned the emancipated fugitive slaves fomenting a massive slave revolt in South Carolina that would bring that colony back into the Spanish imperial orbit.

The evidence seems to demonstrate that the blacks had more human dignity and value under Spanish rule. Spaniards were willing to provide emancipation and manumission—for whatever reasons—and to incorporate blacks into militia units with their own officers. Although in their hierarchical conception of society they saw themselves superior to the black, the white Spaniards still recognized the Negro as a human being with a soul. Conversion to the Catholic faith made him a religious equal in the eyes of God. While the Spaniards exploited and segregated the blacks, they at least gave them some dignity, some value beyond that of hewers of wood and drawers of water. By contrast, in South Carolina the black slave was a chattel without soul or humanity. He was an economic commodity to be bought, sold, and exploited solely for economic ends. One might argue that his situation would have been the same in Florida if the Spanish had produced rice, indigo, and tobacco, but the evidence must stand. The English agent who asserted that slaves were like ships run aground in Florida waters stands out as an example of English attitudes toward their slaves and of man's inhumanity to man.

Pipesmoke and Muskets: Florida Indian Intrigues of the Revolutionary Era

HELEN HORNBECK TANNER

PIPESMOKE and muskets signify peace and war, interrelated aspects of eighteenth-century life for Florida Indians and their neighbors. Pipesmoke refers to peaceful Indian activities—the congresses where passing the pipe was an important ritual. Muskets stand for warfare and hunting. Guns and ammunition had become necessities for American Indians by the Revolutionary Era, used in dealing with enemies and for procuring food and the hides to trade for manufactured articles.

The Florida Indians and their neighbors were involved in a complex pattern of events during the era of the American Revolution. This is the story of "behind scenes" activity, mentioned only briefly in most accounts of the Revolution. The actual or potential behavior of the Indians, particularly the Creeks, was always of serious concern to statesmen, military men, and a frequently alarmed civilian population scattered in isolated communities along the southern frontier.

The time span for this small segment of southern Indian history is 1774 through 1790. This covers the time from the First Continental Congress through the southern military campaigns of the American Revolution which ended with the British surrender of Pensacola in 1781 and the evacuation of Savannah in 1782. It also includes the postwar era, a critical period for the southern Indian and for white Americans, culminating in the inauguration of constitutional government in March 1789 and the first federal treaty with the Creeks in August 1790.

The Florida and Georgia Indians who played a role in the Revo-

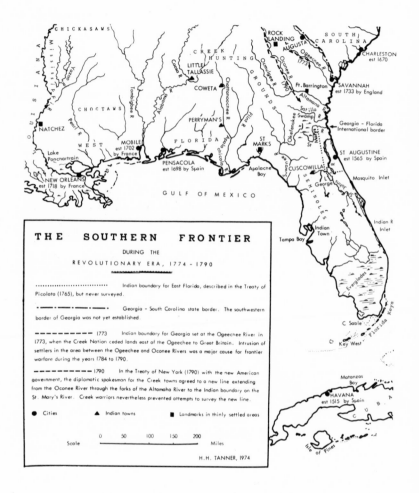

THE   SOUTHERN   FRONTIER

DURING   THE

REVOLUTIONARY   ERA,   1774 - 1790

··························· Indian boundary for East Florida, described in the Treaty of Picolata (1765), but never surveyed.

▪ ▪▪▪ ▪ ▪▪▪ ▪ ▪▪▪ ▪ Georgia – South Carolina state border. The southwestern border of Georgia was not yet established.

— — — — — — — 1773   Indian boundary for Georgia set at the Ogeechee River in 1773, when the Creek Nation ceded lands east of the Ogeechee to Great Britain. Intrusion of settlers in the area between the Ogeechee and Oconee Rivers was a major cause for frontier warfare during the years 1784 to 1790.

— — — — — — — 1790   In the Treaty of New York (1790) with the new American government, the diplomatic spokesman for the Creek towns agreed to a new line extending from the Oconee River through the forks of the Altamaha River to the Indian boundary on the St. Mary's River. Creek warriors nevertheless prevented attempts to survey the new line.

● Cities   ▲ Indian towns   ▪ Landmarks in thinly settled areas

Scale   0   50   100   150   200
                                                    Miles

H.H. TANNER, 1974

lutionary scene were the Creeks and their new Florida branch, the Seminoles. Probably the clearest indication of the importance of these tribes was the territory they controlled. Peninsular Florida was entirely theirs except for a small section of the northeast Atlantic coast about twenty-five miles wide, extending ninety miles south of the St. Marys River between the St. Johns River and the sea.[1] St. Augustine, in existence for more than two centuries, was still the only town in this area. The division between white and Indian territory in East Florida had been established in 1765 by a Creek treaty concluded at Picolata, a small outlying fortification on the St. Johns River west of St. Augustine. This treaty also reaffirmed British rights to the tidewater area along the coast, originally granted by Chief Tomochichi in the first Creek negotiations with the British in Georgia in 1734.

North of the St. Marys River in Georgia, the Creeks had relinquished a coastal strip about forty or fifty miles wide.[2] The upper Ogeechee River marked the dividing line between white and Indian territory. Although Georgia had a significant rural population, the two important urban areas were Augusta—the entrepôt for the Indian trade—located about 100 miles inland at the head of navigation on the Savannah River, and the port town of Savannah. On the opposite side of the Creek country, the small Gulf coast settlement of Pensacola was hemmed in by Indian neighbors, and was vulnerable to attack from Choctaws as well as Creeks. Thus, the Indians still controlled the interior of the Georgia-Florida territory, the south Atlantic coastline, and the Gulf coast past Apalache Bay and the peninsula at the mouth of the Apalachicola River.

A comparison of white and Indian population figures for Florida in the 1770s also indicates the importance of the Creeks and Seminoles. The British inhabitants of West Florida described themselves as a community protected only by 100 men, living within reach of 10,000 Indian warriors.[3] Before the American Revolution,

1. Grant to Gage, Jan. 13, 1766, and Stuart to Gage, Jan. 21, 1766, enclosing Proceedings of Congress at Picolata, Gage Papers, American Series, vol. 47, William L. Clements Library, Ann Arbor. The treaty line was never surveyed.

2. Oglethorpe's treaty with the Creeks, 1734. See also John R. Alden, *John Stuart and the Southern Colonial Frontier, 1754–1775*, University of Michigan Publications in History and Political Science, vol. 15 (Ann Arbor, 1944), map, p. 178. A new Creek boundary in Georgia was set at the Congress of Augusta in November 1763.

3. Memorial of Merchants Trading to West Florida, Nov. 15, 1768, Gage

East Florida had about 1,000 whites and possibly 3,000 Negroes. Most of these whites were not British, but Greeks, Italians, and Minorcans who had come to the New Smyrna colony in 1767.[4] The Florida Seminoles at this time probably numbered more than 1,500, and there were remnants of other tribes living further south on the peninsula, out of contact with the British administration.[5]

Georgia's population was estimated at 25,000 whites, but this total split into Patriot and Loyalist factions with the outbreak of the American Revolution.[6] When the war began, the Upper and Lower Creeks probably numbered at least 15,000 and were counted as having from 3,500 to 5,000 gunmen.[7] To be sure, all the Creek gunmen seldom joined in any single engagement, but the possible participation of several thousand Indian warriors was a military factor that could not be ignored by opposing strategists when the war began.

On the eve of the Revolution, the Creeks and Seminoles were preoccupied with the two basic problems confronting all Indians living on the Anglo frontier: getting sufficient European merchandise, particularly ammunition, and protecting their hunting lands from the encroachment of aggressive white settlers. Trade was the major problem in Florida at that moment; land was the critical issue in Georgia.

The Indian trading situation reached a crisis in Florida early in 1774. A party of angry young Seminole warriors had raided the storehouse of a trader, apparently after a personal disagreement. This incident, adding to reports of Creek hostility in Georgia, persuaded the governor of East Florida to order all trade with the Creeks and Seminoles cut off in mid-February.[8] Anxious to avoid war and to restore trade, representative chiefs went to St. Augustine

---

Papers, English Series, vol. 13. Creeks initially limited the British to settlements occupied by the French and Spanish, but later ceded a strip ten miles wide between Pensacola and Mobile. David H. Corkran, *The Creek Frontier 1540–1783* (Norman, Okla., 1967), p. 248.

4. Charles Loch Mowat, *East Florida as a British Province, 1763–1784*, University of California Publications in History, vol. 32 (Berkeley, 1943; facsimile edition, Gainesville, 1964), pp. 64, 137.

5. John R. Swanton, *Early History of the Creek Indians and their Neighbors*, Bureau of American Ethnology Bulletin 73 (Washington, 1922), p. 440.

6. John R. Alden, *The South in the Revolution, 1763–1789* (Baton Rouge, 1957), p. 9.

7. Swanton, *Creek Indians*, pp. 438, 442.

8. Mowat, *British Province*, p. 24.

in June for a council and peace treaty with the new British governor, Patrick Tonyn. The elders agreed to offer satisfaction for the
damages, and tension eased throughout the Florida Indian country.[9]

The largest celebration of renewed contact between the Indians
and traders was unintentionally staged by the Long Warrior from
the Chiaha village. He had taken a string of horses to trade at St.
Augustine and was returning home with his party of forty warriors,
some women, and twenty five-gallon kegs of "spirits." He planned
to pick up blankets, shirts, and other supplies at the newly reopened
Indian store near present-day Palatka, in preparation for a summer
campaign against the Choctaw. Near the Indian store he met a
party of young traders and packhorse men who persuaded the
Creek warriors to uncork one of the kegs. This began what was
undoubtedly one of the most unrestrained bacchanalian revels ever
to take place on the shores of the St. Johns River. The Long Warrior maintained his equilibrium better than the lesser members of
his tribe and ultimately gathered his band for the trip back toward
the Chattahoochee River.[10]

Peace terms and new trading regulations drawn up in St. Augustine were formally approved during the summer of 1774 with pipe-
smoking ceremonies in the village squares at Cuscowilla, the Seminole town on the Alachua prairie, and at Talahasochte on the
Suwannee River near modern Manatee Springs. In addition to these
trading substations, another Indian store was established below
Lake George, not far from the band of Yuchis living near Spring
Garden.[11] The Seminole nation was still in a formative stage, and
each of these towns maintained jurisdiction over its own affairs.

A decade earlier, only the Indians at Alachua had been called
"wild" or "Seminoles," and the British governor observed during
the Revolutionary Era that this group was still in awe of the lordly
Creeks.[12] Chief Cowkeeper, who welcomed the new British traders
to his Alachua headquarters in 1774, was well known for his hatred
of the Spaniards. His household included a retinue of Yamasee
slaves he had captured in his youth on British-led expeditions

9. William Bartram, *The Travels of William Bartram,* ed. Francis Harper
(New Haven, 1958), pp. 51–52.
10. Ibid., pp. 161–62.
11. Ibid., p. 63.
12. Stuart to Gage, Dec. 26, 1767, enclosing George Roupel to Stuart, Dec.
10, 1767, Gage Papers, American Series, vol. 73. See also Tonyn to Taitt, Mar.
30, 1776, Clinton Papers, Clements Library, Ann Arbor.

against Indian towns under Spanish protection. His community also included Indians who spoke and understood Spanish. As part of their personal decorations they often wore Christian crosses, surviving evidence of the Spanish missions in Florida.[13] Seminoles and Creeks of the Revolutionary Era were aware that their warriors had cooperated with British soldiers in the two great holocausts of the early eighteenth century that virtually destroyed the original tribes of north Florida and coastal Georgia. The first of these catastrophes was the destruction of the Spanish missions in the Apalache district, accomplished mainly within a few months in 1704.[14] The second was the suppression of the Yamasee uprising that broke out along the Savannah River in 1715.[15]

The British trading party to Talahasochte in the summer of 1774 received a reception as cordial as the traders had found at Cuscowilla. The feast preceding the council included barbecued bear ribs, corn cake, honeyed water, and the ceremonial "black drink." Presiding over the entire program was the dignified White King with his symbol of authority, a standard decorated with white buzzard feathers.[16] In spite of the show of good will to the new traders, the Creeks in the vicinity of the Suwannee River were not totally dependent on the British for supplies. Immediately after the Yamasee War of 1715, Creek towns on the Oconee and Ogeechee rivers moved west to the Chattahoochee River; some settled on the lower course specifically to be able to trade with the Spaniards.[17] Although the Floridas had been transferred from Spanish to British rule by the Treaty of Paris in 1763, Cuban fishing vessels carrying trade goods still came annually to the west coast of Florida. Talahasochte was one of the contact points for trading; another was the town on Tampa Bay.[18] In 1774 Spanish merchandise reached Coweta, the principal town of the Lower Creeks.[19]

Reports of Spanish activities among the Creeks had worried

13. Bartram, *Travels*, pp. 117–19.
14. Swanton, *Creek Indians*, pp. 120–23.
15. Ibid., pp 97–100.
16. Ibid., pp. 148–49.
17. Ibid., p. 225.
18. Bartram, *Travels*, pp. 143–44. Bernard Romans, *A Concise Natural History of East and West Florida* (New York, 1775; facsimile edition, Gainesville, 1962), pp. 186–88. See also James W. Covington, "Trade Relations between Southwestern Florida and Cuba, 1660–1840," *Florida Historical Quarterly* 38 (1959):114–28.
19. Stuart to Gage, Jan. 18, 1775, enclosing Samuel Thomas to Taitt, Dec. 10, 1774, Gage Papers, American Series, vol. 125.

British officials for several years.[20] In 1774, however, they felt generally reassured that the Indian trade crisis was resolved and peace
preserved in Florida. Further north in Georgia the frontier was in a
furor over white encroachment on Creek hunting lands. Many
Creeks were not reconciled to the 1773 cession—called the "new
purchase"—of land located higher on the Ogeechee River. Traders
had demanded 2 million acres in payment for debts.[21] During the
boundary survey in 1774, a sagacious Creek caught the official
surveyor trying to point the compass in a direction that would
have marked off more land than had been ceded.[22] During the
spring isolated attacks were reported and several murders committed by partisans of both sides. One of the most unfortunate incidents was the death of Mad Turkey, a Creek chief attached to the
British. He was killed on the street in Augusta by an enraged blacksmith who met him with a jug of rum in one hand and an iron bar
in the other. Although the blacksmith was arrested, he was released
at nightfall by friends who broke into the jail. In the hostilities that
followed such incidents, the Creeks defeated the Georgia militia.
This caused panic in the back country and precipitous flight by the
frontier settlers.

To retaliate, British Indian Superintendent John Stuart sent supplies to the Choctaws to support their fight with the Creeks. He
sent another agent to hinder reconciliation between the Creeks and
Chickasaws. In effect, he promoted intertribal warfare in order to
diminish pressure on the white frontier. The Lower Creek agent,
David Taitt, wanted to bring the chiefs to Savannah for a council,
but the Cherokee thwarted this peace move by warning the Creeks
not to fall under the power of the British.[23]

An alternative solution to the Creek difficulties was undertaken
in 1744 by the Mortar, an anti-British chief who still cherished the

20. Among the documents referring to Spanish-Creek contacts are the following from the Gage Papers: (1) Gage to Stuart, Oct. 12, 1768, including
the statement "I have it in command from His Majesty to desire that you will
pay strictest attention to correspondence between Spaniards and the Creeks,"
vol. 81; (2) Gage to Hillsborough, Sept. 7, 1768, and Brown to Haldimand,
Aug. 14, 1768, vol. 13; (3) Stuart to Gage, Dec. 6, 1768, vol. 14; (4) Gage to
Shelbourne, April 24, 1768, vol. 12; (5) Gage to Stuart, June 25, 1770, vol. 93;
(6) Stuart to Gage, Dec. 14, 1771, vol. 108; (7) Gage to Barrington, Mar. 4,
1772, vol. 21; (8) John Stuart to Gage, May 12, 1774, enclosing Charles
Stuart to Haldimand, May 13, 1773, vol. 119.
21. Alden, John Stuart, pp. 304–5; Bartram, Travels, pp. 205–6.
22. Bartram, Travels, p. 26.
23. Stuart to Gage, May 12, 1774, Gage Papers, vol. 119.

memory of his friendly contact with French officials at Fort Toulouse, an outpost near the Upper Creeks, maintained from 1715 to
1764, the end of the French dominion.[24] In the late fall of 1774,
the Mortar headed a group of eighty Upper Creeks who descended
the Alabama River to meet Lower Creeks and form a delegation to
go to New Orleans to find French officials in the Spanish service.
Through these contacts they hoped to place themselves under the
protection of the King of France and secure French assistance in
driving both the Spaniards and the British out of Creek territory.
In view of the current European situation, this was a quixotic
scheme. The Mortar's followers never reached New Orleans; they
dispersed after the Mortar was fatally injured when hostile Choctaws intercepted their march.[25]

As this account indicates, British colonial politics were not the
primary concern of the Creeks and Seminoles at the beginning of
the American Revolution. On September 7, 1775, at the square in
the Osichi village, the colonial rebellion was presented to Lower
Creek chiefs in the simplest terms through a message from a Patriot
body, the Georgia Council of Safety. The "talk" explained that the
great king across the sea demanded more money from the colonists
than they could afford to pay, and the king had sent his soldiers to
secure more money. Even while this talk was being interpreted, a
message arrived from the deposed royal governor of Georgia, Sir
James Wright, and was immediately relayed to the assembly. The
Lower Creeks replied that they did not wish to become involved in
this quarrel, but hoped it would be settled soon. They wanted only
to keep open the "white road of trade" to their towns. Royalist
sympathy among the Creeks was probably bolstered by the fact
that thirteen horseloads of ammunition had reached the Lower
Creek towns the previous day. Yet, not all towns were equally
satisfied with their shares. Supplies for the Upper Creeks arrived
later from Pensacola. The Upper Creeks were also disinclined to
take part in the British colonial quarrel, sending word that they
would drop their present disputes and join as one man to fight the
enemy if His Majesty were at war with the French or Spaniards.[26]

24. Swanton, *Creek Indians*, p. 196. For the career of the Mortar, see
Corkran, *Creek Frontier*, p. 183.
25. Stuart to Gage, Jan. 18, 1775, Gage Papers, vol. 125.
26. Taitt to Stuart, Sept. 20, 1775, Lower Creeks to Stuart, Sept. 29, 1775,
Clinton Papers.

In spite of the majority sentiment for neutrality at the outset of the American Revolution, total nonparticipation was impossible for the Creeks and Seminoles. George Galphin, who had been licensed to trade in the leading Lower Creek town, Coweta, pulled out of the Indian country in 1775. He immediately became Indian commissioner under the authority of the Continental Congress.[27] After departing, he sent word that his "sons and nephews" would be supplied with goods to carry on trade "as usual." David Holmes, identified as one of Galphin's nephews, was present at the conclave in Osichi square on September 7, 1774. Another nephew was Timothy Barnard, trader on the upper Flint River. Both men later entered the British service.[28] According to Woodward, who sometimes collected rumor as well as fact, Galphin had three families—white, black, and red.[29] Two Indian sons, John and George Galphin, grew to manhood during the American Revolution and played significant roles in tribal affairs by 1787. At the beginning of the Revolution, Galphin's emissaries penetrated Creek and Seminole territory. One of the better known agents was Daniel McMurphy, whom the Indians called "Yellow Hair." As a result of Galphin's efforts, some of the Creeks from Coweta and Hitchiti attended a Patriot-sponsored Indian congress in Augusta in 1776.[30]

The British did not agree on a course of action toward the Creeks. Indian Superintendent John Stuart fled from Charleston to St. Augustine in the summer of 1775 and advised the Creeks and Seminoles to stay out of the war.[31] In 1776, after Stuart had moved on to Pensacola, Governor Tonyn of East Florida tried to engage the Indians in the British cause. He declared that the Americans were ten times more afraid of Indians than they were of any European army.[32] Even with the trading treaty at St. Augustine in 1774, Tonyn feared attack through the Indian country behind St. Augus-

27. Alden, *South in the Revolution*, p. 275; Swanton, *Creek Indians*, p. 226. Galphin was influential until his death in 1780.

28. Taitt to Stuart, Sept. 20, 1775, Clinton Papers; Corkran, *Creek Frontier*, pp. 166, 290, 299, 315.

29. Thomas S. Woodward, *Woodward's Reminiscences of the Creek, or Muscogee Indians* (Montgomery, Ala., 1859; facsimile edition with introduction by Peter Brannon, Tuscaloosa, 1939), p. 105.

30. Taitt to Tonyn, May 3, 1776, Clinton Papers.

31. William Campbell to Gage, July 1, 1775, Gage Papers, vol. 131; Alden, *South in the Revolution*, p. 270.

32. Tonyn to Taitt, March 30, April 20, 1776; Tonyn to Clinton, June 8, 1776 (private), Clinton Papers.

tine once a state of war existed. As a precaution, he issued orders forbidding anyone to cross the St. Johns River without special permission or to leave boats and canoes on the west side of San Sebastian River, a stream flowing half a mile distant around the edge of St. Augustine.[33]

One of the more risky secret missions of the early Revolutionary Era in Florida—and one that required Indian cooperation—was carried out by Thomas Brown, a Loyalist who had been tarred and feathered in Augusta in 1775 and who by 1776 was head of a Loyalist mounted corps, the East Florida Rangers. He set out from St. Augustine in 1776 to smuggle twenty horseloads of ammunition through the Seminole and Creek lands to back-country Loyalists in South Carolina. At Alachua he found that Galphin's agent had preceded him but had not secured any support. The Seminoles were urged to pick up presents left for them on the Altamaha River. These gifts were probably bait set by a persistent "Liberty Man" named Johnathan Bryan who had been trying for several years to secure a land concession from the Creeks. Thomas Brown made his way in safety as far as Coweta. Here he realized that the Creeks were low on ammunition and might refuse to let his pack train proceed. He also knew that their reluctance would be greater if they knew these supplies were for whites, no matter what their political persuasion. After negotiating for several days, he secured the assent of the Pumpkin King and other leaders; they provided an escort through the upper country. The Pumpkin King was on friendly terms with Governor Tonyn.[34]

Actual military participation of the Creeks and Seminoles was negligible in the early years of the Revolutionary War. A powerful deterrent to fighting was the example of the Cherokees who were beaten decisively when they attacked Carolina colonists in 1776.[35] In 1777 about fifty Seminoles and Lower Creeks, headed by Cowkeeper and Perryman, accompanied the East Florida Rangers on an expedition that captured an American post on the Satilla River. They also drove off 2,000 head of cattle. At the beginning of the war, Brown had recommended driving off the cattle of prominent Georgia Patriots in order to feed the British army in St. Augustine.

33. Mowat, *British Province*, p. 109.
34. Brown to Tonyn, May 2, May [8], 1776, both enclosed in Tonyn to Clinton, June 8, 1776, Clinton Papers.
35. Alden, *South in the Revolution*, pp. 272–73.

He even furnished a list of names, headed by George Galphin, who had 3,000 to 4,000 head of cattle at his trading headquarters on the Ogeechee River.[36] The cattle-driving forays into Georgia were considered successful by the British, even though the Indians seem to have acquired considerable herds for themselves. Only ten Indians accompanied the expedition that captured Fort Barrington on the Altamaha River in March 1778.[37]

Brown had confidently expected to raise 1,500 or even 3,000 Creek warriors, but only 80 or 100 ever participated in any of the early British engagements. After Augusta fell to the British in January 1779, Upper and Lower Creeks attacked settlements on the Savannah River. They retired rapidly after their encampment received a surprise attack from a Patriot force in late March. In mid-April a small contingent of about 100 Upper and Lower Creeks advanced with the British army to the vicinity of Charleston. According to a report of the expedition, the Indians behaved extremely well, better than the Georgia Loyalists who committed "shocking" outrages and set an unfortunate example by capturing Negroes as plunder. Even though the mission was successful, the Creeks became uneasy and wanted to return home.[38]

The number of Creek adherents to the British cause increased during the summer of 1779, partially as a result of British military victories at Savannah and Augusta but also in response to the direct efforts of new British agents among the southern tribes. British Indian Superintendent John Stuart, who had been reluctant to mobilize Indian warriors, died in Pensacola on March 21, 1779. A self-appointed board of commissioners with a more aggressive policy took over his responsibilities on March 30, and submitted its own appointments to Crown authorities in England along with reports of local developments.[39] Attention to the provincial Indian situation could not await the delay of months required for an exchange of communications with England, particularly when West Florida

36. Brown to Stuart, Feb. 24, 1776, Clinton Papers.

37. Mowat, *British Province*, pp. 120–21.

38. Summary of heads of letter, Taitt to Clinton, June 11, 1779, Clinton Papers.

39. The commissioners who succeeded John Stuart in directing Indian affairs in West Florida for an interim period were Andrew Rainsford, John Mitchell, Alexander Macullough, David Holmes, and Robert Taitt: Board of Indian Commissioners to Lords Commissioner of Treasury (duplicate), July 14, 17, 1779, Intercepted Letters 1779–81, 2:9, 40. M247 Roll 65, National Archives Microfilm Publication (1958).

seemed in danger of American attack by way of the Ohio and Mississippi river valleys.

The commissioners' first official instructions arrived on May 26 in a communication from Lord George Germain to John Stuart, written in December 1778. Stuart was ordered to dismiss his Creek agents, David Taitt and William McIntosh, because Governor Tonyn had registered strong objection to their activities. The executor of Stuart's estate refused to give the commissioners access to the late superintendent's official papers, so they had no knowledge of the background or the basis of the charges against Taitt and McIntosh. Carrying out Germain's instructions as well as they could, they dispatched one of their members, David Holmes, to the Lower Creek country with a circular letter dated March 30, 1779, informing Taitt and McIntosh that they were dismissed from the Indian service and enjoined from interfering with the management of the Indians.[40] Apparently Holmes found Taitt, for on June 11 Taitt wrote General Clinton that he believed his authority as a deputy under Stuart had ceased.[41]

Holmes' fellow commissioners were aware of his previous connection with Patriot George Galphin, and they respected his thorough knowledge of the Creek country and considerable influence within the tribe. After taking the dismissal notices to Taitt and McIntosh, he was directed to proceed to Augusta and establish headquarters there. He was also expected to gather parties of Creeks and whites to serve under Augustine Prevost and Archibald Campbell in the British southern campaigns, taking care that the Indians did not attack frontier settlers supporting the British generals.[42] Holmes was not working alone. Of the subsidiary members of the Indian staff in Lower Creek territory, probably the most important was the commissary, Timothy Barnard, who supplied the Indians with trade goods.[43]

By July 1779, Upper Creek towns were openly expressing their sympathy for the British, quite possibly because they were no

40. Board of Indian Commissioners to David Taitt and William McIntosh, May 30, 1779, ibid., pp. 49–50.
41. Taitt to Clinton, June 11, 1779, Clinton Papers.
42. Board of Indian Commissioners to David Holmes, May 30, 1779, Intercepted Letters, 2:53–54.
43. Indian Department, Abstract of Receipts, April 14 to June 30, 1779, includes quarterly salary for Timothy Barnard, Commissary of Indian Affairs for Lower Creeks; George Nowlan, Assistant Commissary; and Edward Haynes, Interpreter, ibid., p. 127.

longer able to get supplies from American traders. Chiefs and headmen of the Great Tallassie town previously had been attached to the Americans, but they came to Pensacola to renew their friendship with the British and "forget the past." A succession of warriors arrived in town to recount their exploits and enjoy the hospitality of the volunteer Indian commissioners. Holmes sent word in early July that he anticipated reaching General Prevost with several hundred Creeks, and with additional parties to follow. Throughout the Creek country, towns planned to send out re-inforcements in late July after the annual "busk," the summer Green Corn Festival celebrated by all the southern Indians.[44]

Although the Indian commissioners in Pensacola concentrated their major efforts on the Creeks living along the Georgia-Florida frontier, they continued to maintain agents among the other southern tribes. On May 20, shortly before receiving the orders from Lord Germain, they issued instructions to Alexander Cameron, veteran deputy superintendent among the Cherokees, who at that point was returning to his station in Carolina. Cameron, commander of a company of Loyal Refugees, was instructed to take a large body of Indian warriors to the frontiers of Georgia and South Carolina to serve under British leaders.[45] John McIntosh, British commissary for the Chickasaws, was provided with presents for the chiefs of that tribe when he returned to his station on the northwestern frontier of West Florida.[46] During the American Revolution the Chickasaws were an important source of intelligence because of their daily contact with Shawnee messengers from Ohio who brought information from the northern tribes of the Great Lakes region.[47]

On June 12, 1779, the commissioners delegated another of their members, Robert Taitt, to take messages and presents to the Choctaws. Taitt was sent first to Mobile to contact a man named Bethune, his guide to the Choctaws.[48] This was a potentially hazardous assignment. The British in Pensacola feared the Spanish agents

44. Board of Indian Commissioners to Lord George Germain (duplicate no. 6), July 12, 1779, ibid., pp. 17–22.

45. Instructions to Alexander Cameron, May 20, 1779, ibid., p. 61.

46. Board of Commissioners to Lords Commissioner of the Treasury, July 17, 1779, ibid., p. 11.

47. Talk of the Chickasaws to the Rebels, May 1779, ibid., pp. 41–42.

48. Instructions to Robert Taitt, June 12, 1779, ibid., p. 57. The anticipated guide to the Choctaw was probably Ferquahar Bethune, later deputy agent for the Mississippi district.

from New Orleans who were influential in the Choctaw towns. On the surface, relations between British West Florida and Spanish Louisiana appeared cordial, but by July 1779, governors of both provinces were anticipating war. Spain was expected to join her Bourbon ally, France, who had entered the revolutionary conflict against England in 1778. Spain had declared war on England in May 1779, and a council of war was in progress in Cuba in mid-July, but official news did not reach Bernardo de Gálvez, governor of Louisiana, until August. He chose to keep this development and his own promotion a secret until his military offensive was under way on August 27. In order to keep news of war preparations from reaching British Pensacola, Governor Gálvez apprehended Bethune without explanation and held him in custody when he came to Louisiana, ostensibly on personal business, in late August.[49] By the time the British in Pensacola became aware of Spain's entry into the Revolution, Gálvez' forces had already seized British outposts on the Mississippi River and had laid plans for taking the forts at Mobile and Pensacola.

Although the endeavors of the self-appointed Pensacola Indian commissioners cannot be evaluated with any precision, it seems evident that the British on the southern front had acquired additional Indian support—particularly among the Creeks—even before Gálvez commenced operations on the Gulf coast. The authority of the commissioners ended in the fall of 1779 when news arrived that Lord George Germain had appointed two superintendents in the southern district to replace John Stuart. Alexander Cameron became superintendent for the western section toward the Mississippi River, including the Choctaws and Chickasaws. Colonel Thomas Brown of the East Florida Rangers was placed in charge of the Creeks, Cherokees, and Catawbas as superintendent for the eastern district. Both assignments were for military service in support of the British army. In conjunction with the appointments, Germain dispatched vessels with Indian supplies to Georgia and to Pensacola.[50]

At the beginning of the Revolution, the Creek chiefs had indicated that they would join the British cause if the French or Spanish became involved. By late 1779, both European nations were

49. John Walton Caughey, *Bernardo de Gálvez in Louisiana, 1776–1783* (Berkeley, 1934), pp. 151, 182 ff.

50. Germain to Clinton, #41, June 25, 1779, enclosing copy of Germain to Thomas Brown and Alexander Cameron of same date, Clinton Papers. (Clinton received the letter on Sept. 1 by the packet *Mercury*.)

opposing the British in the southern military theater. The French fleet was operating off the Georgia coast while Gálvez was engaged in his campaign originating in New Orleans. He caught the British completely off guard. In February 1780, Alexander Cameron was planning an Indian congress for March 15 in Mobile to distribute Indian presents sent by the Earl of Bathurst.[51] On March 14, the fort at Mobile surrendered to Gálvez, offering him virtually no opposition. By that time an estimated 1,500 Indians had gathered to augment the British forces at Pensacola where the Spanish were expected to strike next.[52] Major General John Campbell credited the presence of the Creek warriors with deterring the Spanish attack in the spring of 1780. In November, he again begged Colonel Brown to send Creek re-inforcements speedily because the long delayed Spanish invasion was about to begin.[53] The Indian auxiliaries—Creeks, Seminoles, Choctaws, and some Chickasaws—played a major role in the British defense of Pensacola, which was besieged by a Spanish naval force and land expedition beginning in March 1781. Journal accounts of the siege mention a "score of times" when Indian parties engaged in skirmishes, returning with weapons and prisoners, but sometimes only with scalps. Pensacola surrendered on May 10, 1781, after a lucky Spanish shot exploded the powder magazine inside the British fort. Gálvez later observed that the Indians were the best defense the British had, and consequently issued orders offering friendship and adequate trading facilities immediately.[54]

After the fall of Pensacola, some Creeks aided Colonel Brown in defending Augusta against American attack until Brown was forced to surrender on June 6, 1781.[55] Emistisiguo, great leader of the Upper Creeks, was killed in combat outside Savannah before the British evacuated the town in July 1782, in the last major engagement of the American Revolution on the Georgia coast.[56]

The Treaty of Paris in 1783 formally concluded hostilities between the European antagonists in the American Revolution and

51. Gen. John Campbell to Clinton, Feb. 10, 1780, Letterbook 3, p. 128, Clinton Papers.
52. Caughey, *Bernardo de Gálvez*, pp. 189–90.
53. Gen. John Campbell to Brown, Nov. 15, 1780 (extract), Clinton Papers.
54. Caughey, *Bernardo de Gálvez*, pp. 210–11.
55. Kenneth Coleman, *The American Revolution in Georgia, 1763–1789* (Athens, 1958), pp. 131–35.
56. Ibid., p. 144; Alden, *South in the Revolution*, p. 278; Corkran, *Creek Frontier*, pp. 321–22.

proclaimed the independence of the thirteen American colonies, but the basis for strife persisted in the Georgia-Florida Indian country. The contest for Creek land, suppressed during the war years, immediately emerged as a major issue. Reacting to Creek opposition during the war, Georgia called a "peace" congress in Augusta in October 1783. The few Creeks present were unexpectedly pressured to sign a treaty ceding their lands as far west as the Oconee River. The fraudulent treaty was the beginning of a chain of events that led to the Treaty of New York in 1790 in which Indian title to the contested hunting land was finally relinquished. Chiefs of only two towns signed the Treaty of Augusta in 1783, later claiming that their lives would have been in danger if they had refused. Following the "peace" congress, any Indian who came to Augusta to trade was exhorted to add his cross mark acknowledging the treaty.[57]

The peace settlement at the end of the Revolution also thrust the Creeks into a contest between the United States and Spain. Diplomats in Paris in 1783 reassigned sovereignty over the Creek tribal territory, returning East and West Florida to Spain with an uncertain boundary between Spain and the United States extending from the Mississippi River to the undetermined western boundary of Georgia.[58] Furthermore, the end of the Revolution did not eliminate the British from Creek affairs. British Loyalists remaining in East Florida strongly influenced the Indian policy of the incoming Spanish administration. In these circumstances, plots and Indian intrigue intensified in the Georgia-Florida region during the immediate postwar years. In the background were the personal objectives of Creek chiefs, traders, land speculators, adventurers, and officials of Spain, Great Britain, Georgia, and the United States.

The key figure in the subsequent Indian intrigues of Georgia and Florida was the leader of the Creek contingent at the siege of Pensacola, the talented mixed-blood chief Alexander McGillivray. In addition to his native ability, McGillivray understood the system

57. McGillivray to O'Neill, March 28, 1786; McGillivray to Miró, May 1, 1786, in John Walton Caughey, *McGillivray of the Creeks* (Norman, Okla., 1938), pp. 105–6.

58. The border controversy was settled in one of the provisions of the Treaty of San Lorenzo in 1795. Americans insisted on 31 degrees latitude, the present northern boundary of Florida west of the St. Marys River. Spain claimed the boundary established by the British for West Florida, 32 degrees and 8 minutes. The difference amounted to a band of territory 70 miles wide.

the Indians were opposing. He had left the Creek country for Charleston in 1773. Under the guidance of his father, Lachlan Mc-Gillivray, and a minister uncle, the Reverend Farquar McGillivray, he had three years of intensive education and accounting experience in Savannah before the Revolution ended his formal training. He returned to his Creek home in 1776 when his father, prominent Loyalist and Indian trader, returned to Scotland. Little Tallasie on the Coosa River in modern Alabama was his headquarters until his death in 1793 at the age of thirty-four. His ingrained antipathy for Georgians was heightened by the confiscation of his father's estate, valued at $100,000. During the Revolution, McGillivray served as British commissary among the Upper Creeks. He rarely joined a war party, but in March 1779 was involved in fighting along the Savannah River.[59]

McGillivray made the initial overtures toward securing Spanish political support and continued British trade for the Creeks as soon as he learned the terms of the definitive peace treaty in late 1783. His own letters and supporting correspondence circulated through the Spanish administrative hierarchy, ultimately achieving his objective. After the Spanish conquest of Pensacola in 1781 and the British evacuation of Savannah in 1782, St. Augustine was the only remaining British entry port for the Creek Indian trade. William Panton, trader and friend of McGillivray's father, and Colonel Thomas Brown, McGillivray's superior officer in the Indian service, were both residents of St. Augustine when the war ended. These staunch Loyalists were the principal sources of information for the new Spanish governor, Vizente Manuel de Zéspedes, who reached Florida in June 1784.[60] Governor Zéspedes approved Panton's application for handling the Creek trade with a Spanish license, a recommendation made repeatedly by McGillivray.

In the first Indian congress of Spaniards and Creeks held at Pensacola on May 31 and June 1, 1784, McGillivray was named Spanish commissary to the Creek nation. The violently anti-Spanish Seminole chief Cowkeeper had died in March 1784, which eased the transfer of Indian affairs from British to Spanish authority in East Florida. The governor held a congress with the Seminoles in September

59. Caughey has written a biographical sketch of McGillivray, pp. 3–57, as an introduction to his publication of McGillivray correspondence.

60. Helen Hornbeck Tanner, *Zéspedes in East Florida, 1784–1790* (Coral Gables, 1963), pp. 79–104, treats the Spanish role in Creek affairs in greater detail.

1784, followed by a larger congress at St. Augustine in December which included Lower Creeks. The Panton, Leslie Company furnished the Indian presents and supplies for these events, a step toward their achievement by 1786 of monopoly of the Indian trade in the Spanish Floridas.[61]

Beginning in 1784, McGillivray managed to extend gradually his control over southern Indian affairs. He was determined to keep Georgia traders out of the Creek country and to prevent further encroachment on the valuable Oconee River hunting lands. Georgians were insisting on recognition of the "treaty" and land cession extorted from the two chiefs in 1783. The blunt tactics of the Georgians were no match for the maneuvers McGillivray carried out through a network of personal contacts in the Creek country and in extensive intertribal communication with other southern and northern tribes. He also carried on a masterful diplomatic correspondence with American and Spanish officials and regularly exchanged intelligence with his friend and business associate William Panton.

With the security of Spanish and British backing, McGillivray wrote forcefully to Georgia Governor John Houston, warning settlers to stay off the Oconee River lands. His threats brought at least formal results. In November 1784 he learned that the governor and the assembly had forbidden settlement of the area.[62] At the same time, he ordered an ambitious Georgia trader named Elijah Clarke to leave the Creek country. Clarke was one of the American leaders who had forced the surrender of Colonel Thomas Brown at Augusta in 1781. McGillivray's eviction notice required time to enforce because Clarke's men were able to waylay Creek hunters and engage in trading before the Creeks reached Panton's depot.[63] McGillivray countered by providing his personal messengers to Panton and to Spanish officials with little paper memos indicating appropriate gifts such as a blanket, shirt, or keg of "taffy." These special favors increased McGillivray's following in the Creek tribe. Coercion was not suitable or even feasible in Indian society.

On the other hand, McGillivray was ruthless in dealing with a group of white men living in the Creek nation and scheming to

61. Caughey, *McGillivray*, doc. 13, pp. 75–77. See also Joseph Byrne Lockey, *East Florida, 1783–1785, a File of Documents Assembled and Many of Them Translated* (Berkeley and Los Angeles, 1949), pp. 280–83, 428–30.
62. Caughey, *McGillivray*, doc. 20, p. 84.
63. Ibid., docs. 18, 19, pp. 80–83.

dominate tribal affairs. This source of trouble was effectively elim-
inated by publicly executing three of the ringleaders.[64] Not all
whites were unwelcome in the Creek country, for Indian traders
and their families had a respected status. Among the approximately
100 Creek and Seminole towns were many chiefs with English or
Scottish names.[65] McGillivray himself was the most outstanding example of the success of a man of Indian and Scottish heritage. His
closest associate in Creek affairs was a Lower Creek chief, Perryman. Cowkeeper's successor among the Seminoles was named
Payne.

Internal affairs of the Creek nation were a subsidiary concern for
Alexander McGillivray. He mainly handled the external affairs of
the Creeks and neighboring tribes. In July 1785, he issued a joint
protest in behalf of Creeks, Cherokees, and Chickasaws, objecting
to American encroachment on all southern Indian lands. This widely
circulated statement of the Indians' case even reached the King of
Spain. Before releasing the strongly worded protest, McGillivray
presented it for approval at the annual meeting where the presiding
official was Mad Dog, chief of the leading Upper Creek town of
Tuckabatchee.[66]

Commissioners representing the American Confederation actively
entered Creek diplomacy in 1785, inviting the chiefs and headmen
to attend a congress at Galphinton on the Ogeechee River in October. They hoped to secure cession of land already illegally settled
by Georgia families. In September, Perryman led a Creek delegation on a quiet excursion to gather preliminary information. The
Creeks first went to Georgia officials in Savannah, then to retiring
British Governor Tonyn on shipboard in St. Marys River harbor
about to sail for England, and finally to Governor Zéspedes in St.
Augustine.[67] They were able to communicate easily with Zéspedes,
assisted by the governor's English-speaking secretary, Captain Carlos Howard of the Irish regiment in the Spanish army. These three
conferences undoubtedly contributed to the Creeks' majority decision not to attend the American-sponsored congress. When commissioners representing the American Confederation and the State

64. Ibid., doc. 5, fn. 10, p. 70.
65. Prominent names were McQueen, McDonald, Kinnaird, Cornell, Galphin,
and Weatherford.
66. Caughey, *McGillivray*, doc. 24, pp. 90–93.
67. Lockey, *East Florida*, pp. 556–62.

of Georgia arrived at Galphinton, they met only twenty warriors with two Upper Creek and two Lower Creek chiefs. The American commissioners immediately withdrew, but the Georgia delegation stayed behind and secured signatures to a treaty from two chiefs, the Tame King of Tallassie and the Fat King of Cussita, leaders of the Lower Creek minority sympathetic to American interests.[68]

At the big meeting of the Lower and Upper Creeks in early April 1786, the nation decided to take the offensive against encroaching American settlers. War parties set out immediately to drive settlers from the Oconee land and to attack settlements at Cumberland and at Muscle Shoals on the Tennessee River. Although the warriors were instructed to prevent loss of American lives, some fatalities were inevitable.[69] Preparing for more extensive hostilities, McGillivray went to Governor Estevan Miró in New Orleans and arranged to have 5,000 pounds of gunpowder provided for Upper Creek warriors, to be distributed secretly through Panton's warehouse in Pensacola so Spanish officials would not be implicated.[70] Governor Zéspedes of East Florida likewise provided 5,000 pounds of powder for the Lower Creeks and agreed to give additional supplies to those Creeks who brought notes from McGillivray. This aid was surreptitious. In his correspondence with Georgia's governor and in statements to inquiring official visitors, Zéspedes convincingly insisted he gave the Creeks supplies only for "hunting."[71]

While McGillivray was in Pensacola in mid-summer 1786, Daniel McMurphy, agent for Georgia at the beginning of the American Revolution, returned to the Creek country on a rather ill-advised mission for the Georgia legislature. McMurphy announced that the Creeks were responsible for ceding the Oconee River land. He also contended that the Creek traders should have licenses from Georgia rather than from McGillivray. Creeks refused to listen until McGillivray arrived to call a meeting, but by that time McMurphy had returned to Georgia. He continued his harassing tactics for several months, offering rewards for McGillivray's murder and plotting the assassinations of McGillivray and certain chiefs

68. *American State Papers, Indian Affairs* (Washington, 1832), 4:17. See also Caughey, *McGillivray,* doc. 33, pp. 102–3; doc. 58, pp. 138–39.

69. Caughey, *McGillivray,* doc. 36, pp. 106–10. This is an important summary.

70. Ibid., doc. 41, pp. 117–18.

71. Zéspedes to Ezpeleta, May 25, Oct. 16, 1786, EF: b2 H2, Lockey Collection, P. K. Yonge Library of Florida History, University of Florida, Gainesville.

and traders. Ultimately, he had to flee to save his own life.[72] In August 1786, the Creeks boldly sent an ultimatum to Georgia demanding that settlers stay off Creek lands. Rather than commencing hostilities at once, they declared a truce for the duration of the winter hunting season.[73]

On October 15, 1786, Georgia again attempted to secure a valid cession of the contested Oconee land at a meeting held on Shoulderbone Creek, with armed troops in attendance.[74] As usual, only the Fat King of Cussita and the Tame King of Tallassie and their followers appeared. The longstanding sympathy of the Cussitas for Americans was probably influenced by the presence of the two sons of George Galphin, the former Creek trader who became Indian commissioner for the Continental Congress and agent for Georgia after retiring from the Indian country in 1775. Exasperated by the poor showing, the Georgians seized members of the pro-American faction, later releasing the chiefs but holding five Indian hostages. These hostages were freed through the intercession of James White, a representative of the American Congress who attended the spring meeting of the Lower Creeks at the Oussitche Square in April 1787. From the information gained at that meeting, White provided the American government with the first reasonable account of the Creek-Georgia land dispute. As a result of the Georgians' foolish move at Shoulderbone Creek, the Cussitas and Tallassies joined other Creek towns in warfare against Georgia in 1787.[75]

By 1787, McGillivray's network of influence spread to the northern Indian tribes. The Upper Creek congress in June 1787 was attended by chiefs of the Mohawks and Oneidas from New York, Wyandots and Shawnees from Michigan and Ohio, and twenty-five other nations from the Great Lakes region. Tribal representatives made joint plans to attack all surveyors, prevent further grants of land, and keep in contact in the future.[76] Contemporary with the Creek-Cherokee war on the southern frontier, the northern Indians were fighting to retain their lands northwest of the Ohio River. With support from the British at Detroit, the confederacy was organizing in the region of the Maumee and Wabash rivers. Chero-

72. Caughey, *McGillivray*, doc. 42, pp. 118–20; doc. 65, p. 147; doc. 67, p. 149.
73. Ibid., doc. 46, pp. 123–24; doc. 54, p. 133.
74. Ibid., doc. 50, pp. 129–30; *American State Papers*, 4:20.
75. Caughey, *McGillivray*, doc. 63, pp. 144–45.
76. Ibid., doc. 70, pp. 153–55; doc. 75, pp. 160–62.

kees had been present at an important meeting on the Detroit River in December 1786.[77] Shawnees fought along with the Creeks in the South.[78] Warfare spread all along the southern frontier. Mc-Gillivray dispatched 500 to 600 warriors to join the Cherokees fighting in the Cumberland region. White settlers again were driven from the contested Oconee land, and every home and outbuilding was burned to the ground. The Upper Creeks initiated hostilities against Georgians who mistakenly retaliated with attacks on the Lower Creeks, which further consolidated the Indian forces. By fall McGillivray declared, "The State of Georgia now lays at our mercy."[79]

After three years of persistent effort, beginning in 1784, McGilli-vray achieved unprecedented unity among the towns of the Creek confederacy. Seminoles also joined in support of his objectives, probably because he had exerted pressure to have supplies for their use brought to a more conveniently located store at St. Marks in Apalache. In April 1787, the Seminoles participated for the first time in the annual meeting of the Lower Creeks.[80] Extending his campaign against Georgia land-grabbing outside his own tribe, McGillivray arranged in 1787 for the murder of a land company agent who was active among the Chickasaws and Choctaws.[81] Within the tribe he was recognized as chief speaker for the Creeks.[82]

But the very success of the Creeks created hazards. In 1788, Spanish officials in Pensacola were hesitant to support an aggressive Indian war against the American states. A flamboyant adventurer from the Bahama Islands, William Augustus Bowles, introduced new complications into the Creek and Seminole country. Bowles, who harbored ambitions to become ruler of the Creek nation, was at the beginning of a dramatic career which ended at Morro Castle, Cuba, in 1806. His venture in Florida was backed by the governor

77. *Michigan Historical Collections* (Lansing, 1888), 11:467. Not many of these intertribal contacts appear in documents. There is a record of a Delaware Indian returning from Pensacola to a British-sponsored congress near Detroit with news of Spaniards: *Michigan Historical Collections* (Lansing, 1895), 24: 263.

78. Caughey, *McGillivray*, doc. 63, p. 145.

79. Ibid., doc. 71, p. 155; doc. 79, p. 167; doc. 78, p. 165.

80. Ibid., doc. 78, pp. 165–66, 167n116. The previous summer, McGil-livray had written, "as for the Semanolies I have but little Acquaintance with the present leaders, the former ones whom I knew are dead" (doc. 47, p. 125).

81. Ibid., doc. 75, p. 160; doc. 80, pp. 169, 134n73.

82. *American State Papers*, 4:36; Caughey, *McGillivray*, doc. 67, p. 150.

of the British Bahamas and by a New Providence trading firm, bitter commercial enemies of Panton, Leslie. Although Bowles tried to conceal his business connections and his personal goal, the vital information reached Governor Zéspedes in West Florida from Colonel Thomas Brown, former British Indian superintendent, who was among the Loyalist refugees living in the Bahama Islands.[83]

Bowles and his party landed on the East Florida coast near Mosquito Inlet in April 1788 and advanced through the Seminole towns to the Apalachicola River. He appeared to the Indians as a "stranger" who promised to send a shipload of presents. Bowles returned by the same overland route across Florida in October. Though many of his followers deserted to the Spanish military post on the St. Johns River, Bowles himself made his way to the Lower Creek town of his father-in-law, McGillivray's trusted friend Perryman. None of the details or explanations reached McGillivray with the first brief report of the stranger's arrival. He discovered upon investigation that Bowles was a soldier he had known in Pensacola during the Revolution. Because of Bowles' relation to Perryman, he was disinclined to overstep the iron-bound customs of Creek hospitality and use violence to get rid of the intruder. When Bowles' deception was partially revealed and the long overdue vessel brought disappointing gifts, the Creeks forced Bowles to leave early in 1789.[84] The mysterious behavior of Bowles created an assortment of rumors and suspicions in Georgia and both Floridas. Most damaging to the Creeks was the unwarranted conclusion drawn by Governor Arturo O'Neill in Pensacola that McGillivray was in league with Bowles and the British against Spain. O'Neill sent his own agent among the Creeks to collect information about McGillivray's activities.[85]

Although McGillivray was successful in maintaining trade and in combatting the schemes of Georgians to acquire additional Creek land, he was ultimately forced to deal with the formidable power of the United States. At first McGillivray had viewed the new inde-

83. Tanner, Zéspedes, pp. 189–95. An important primary document is Substance of a voluntary declaration made by the Bowles Banditti, Nov. 21, 1788, in St. Augustine, Archivo Nacional de Cuba, Florida Correspondence, Leg. 1, Exp. 24 No. 2, transcript, P. K. Yonge Library.

84. For a complete study of Bowles and his attack on the Panton, Leslie store in 1792, see J. Leitch Wright, William Augustus Bowles, Director General of the Creek Nation (Athens, Ga., 1967).

85. Caughey, McGillivray, doc. 107, pp. 205–6.

pendent nation as a "distracted republic" liable to be divided among European rulers.[86] Under the Constitution of 1789, however, the nation appeared destined to survive. The new national government of the United States was determined to deal with the Creeks, not only to create peace for frontier inhabitants, but also to gain Creek cooperation in defeating the schemes of Georgian and private land companies to control land beyond the western limit of the state settlements. McGillivray had been approached and even plagued by agents of land companies who doubted the federal government's claim to jurisdiction over the interior of the country.[87] By establishing friendly relations with the Creeks, the federal government also hoped to diminish Spanish influence in the region disputed by Spain and the United States. Spanish officials had urged McGillivray to make peace with Americans, but not to make any land or trade concessions.

The first overtures of commissioners from the federal government led to a meeting at Rock Landing on the Oconee River in September 1789. John and George Galphin handled preliminary discussions among the Lower Creeks, using their influence in the leading towns of Coweta and Cussita. A peace treaty planned for June was postponed because war sentiment was so strong among the Creeks. Two thousand men were under arms, and 1,500 rifles were expected from Pensacola. At Rock Landing, McGillivray appeared for the first time to negotiate personally with American treaty commissioners. The opening formalities—including the "black drink" ceremony—began on September 21, and three days later the copy of the proposed treaty was handed to McGillivray. After discussing the terms and deciding no agreement could be reached, McGillivray and his Creek delegation simply decamped late in the evening. American demands were unacceptable because they conflicted with his obligations to the Spanish and to Panton. He was also incensed at the "insolence" of one of the commissioners, David Humphrey, a personal protegé of Washington, who supposedly had acquired diplomatic experience during peace talks at Versailles in 1783. From camps at increasing distances from Rock Landing, McGillivray sent back messages that the horses needed better forage,

86. Ibid., doc. 7, p. 70.
87. Ibid., doc. 139, p. 259. This is one of the references to the "Rambling Agents of the Yazoo Companys," who procured provisional grants from Georgia in 1789. See Arthur P. Whitaker, *The Spanish-American Frontier* (Boston and New York, 1927), pp. 125 ff.

that he was "indisposed," and finally that the principal chiefs had departed for winter hunting. The more conciliatory chiefs of the Cussitas remained at Rock Landing to smoke a pipe of peace with their "elder brothers," the Americans. The affronted American commissioners conferred with officials in Augusta before returning to New York. Their official report asserted that Georgia's claims to Creek land were well founded and further recommended that the national government bring an army against the Creeks to force submission.[88]

Senator Benjamin Hawkins of North Carolina became apprehensive about the consequences of the commissioners' unfavorable account of McGillivray's aloof behavior. In the spring of 1790, he sent a personal representative to McGillivray to explain the dangers he faced and the importance of making peace immediately with federal authorities. Hawkins had been a commissioner at the unsuccessful treaty attempt at Galphinton in 1785 and remained definitely interested in the Creek nation. In 1786, he had written privately, announcing plans to move to the Creek frontier and requesting McGillivray to select for him a suitable "Indian damsel" to be his consort.[89]

Persuaded by Hawkins' analysis of the situation, McGillivray and twenty-seven Creeks set off for New York City in June 1790, covering most of the route by stagecoach and wagon. He made this decision in conjunction with Creek chiefs, but without conferring with any of his usual outside advisers. William Panton was in the Chickasaw country, too far away to exchange correspondence, but McGillivray's letter to John Leslie in St. Augustine brought action as soon as the contents were revealed to Governor Zéspedes. Within forty-eight hours, Captain Carlos Howard, the governor's chief assistant, was on shipboard bound for New York on an excursion "for his health." Captain Howard reached port ahead of the Creek party and went down to meet McGillivray in Philadelphia, taking along letters of advice from Leslie and Zéspedes.

Though McGillivray was housed at the home of Henry Knox, secretary of war, he still kept in close contact with Captain Howard throughout the treaty negotiations in New York. Howard

88. *American State Papers*, 4:34–36, 73–79.

89. Caughey, *McGillivray*, doc. 32, p. 102; doc. 138, pp. 256–58. The representative was Colonel Marinus Willet. Hawkins became Creek agent in 1796, serving until after the War of 1812. After McGillivray died in 1793, he was next "beloved man" of the nation.

appeared at his side at all public functions, including a reception at the home of President Washington. The American discomfiture provided McGillivray with many private chuckles. A less conspicuous figure on the scene was George Beckwith, a British naval attaché acting as official observer—Britain did not yet have an accredited diplomatic representative to her former colonies. Beckwith was puzzled by the solicitous attention the Americans accorded McGillivray because he knew that a man named Bowles was on his way from Quebec to England, at British expense, claiming to represent the Creek nation in important matters to be revealed only to the British crown.

The first treaty of peace and friendship between the United States and the Creek nation was signed on August 7, 1790, and publicly celebrated a week later at Federal Hall in the presence of a large assembly of citizens and government officials. After President Washington addressed the Creeks through an interpreter, he presented McGillivray with a string of beads as a peace token and a gift of tobacco to smoke in remembrance. The ceremonies concluded with the Creeks shaking hands with the President and performing a "peace song."[90]

Although the Creeks made land concessions, the treaty was not so much a capitulation as a safety play engineered by their diplomatic representative. McGillivray had learned that England and Spain were on the verge of war over occupation of Nootka Sound on the northwest Pacific coast. Such a conflict could endanger the supply routes of his tribe; they depended on Spanish authorities who allowed British ships to bring goods from the Bahama Islands through the Florida Straits to Pensacola. Although he refused to renounce his Spanish connections, he realized that circumstances might make his nation dependent on American goods and support. The treaty had a secret clause which allowed him two or three years to change trade connections if he desired. He was also assigned a stipend of $1,200 a year, which he considered a partial indemnification for the loss of his father's property in Georgia during the Revolution.[91]

So the contests over land and trade which had originated during the early Revolutionary period in the Florida and Georgia Indian

90. Ibid., doc. 146, p. 276; doc. 147, p. 278; doc. 150, pp. 281–84.
91. George Washington recommended inclusion of the secret clause: *American State Papers*, 4:80–82; Caughey, *McGillivray*, doc. 156, p. 290.

country developed by 1790 to the stage of frock-coated diplomacy in a northern capital. After this date, little could be permanently accomplished for the Creeks and their Indian neighbors by intrigue, plots, or even the most adroit personal endeavors. Lands along the Oconee River were only the first Creek concession to the American government. Relentless population pressure ended the era of alternative warfare and peacemaking. Within two generations the Creeks and their neighbors were forced to move West, except for the adamant Seminoles who made Florida the last frontier east of the Mississippi River.

Commentary

WILLIAM C. STURTEVANT

THE customary and proper duty of an anthropologist commenting on papers by historians is to call attention to cultural factors, especially to the importance of cultural differences, and to put forward a reminder that we should consider those actors in historical events who left no records because they either could not or did not write.

Professor TePaske has explained clearly how and why Spanish Florida became a refuge for escaped slaves from the North. Even though, as he concluded, very few black fugitives from Georgia and Carolina succeeded in reaching Florida as a refuge during the First Spanish Period, the memory of Florida as a refuge must have survived among slaves and slave owners to the north throughout the British period until Florida was returned to Spain after the American Revolution. In the period from 1783 to 1858, the fugitive slaves among the Seminoles in Florida—or the fear among American slave owners of such fugitives—were among the main reasons for, first, the American capture of Florida, and second, the wars against the Seminoles and their eventual deportation to Indian Territory in Oklahoma.

Professor TePaske describes his paper as a comparison and contrast of "the slave policies of the Spanish in Florida and the English in South Carolina, particularly as they affected intercolonial relationships." But there was another party to the intercolonial relationship: the Indian societies, whose slave policies—or, better, black policies—are very much in need of examination. Perhaps especially important are the policies of the Creeks and Seminoles, into or through whose country the slaves fled. Unfortunately, the role of blacks among independent Indians in Florida and the rest of the South is not well represented in the documents, and in subsequent oral tradition (Indian, black, and white) earlier roles and attitudes have been much distorted by later radical shifts in interethnic relations and attitudes.[1]

The late eighteenth and early nineteenth centuries were important for the diffusion of Indian genes and Indian cultural traits into the American black population, and from them, as well as directly, into the general American population. Diffusion in the reverse direction of course took place at this time and later.[2] These topics are in much need of further research.

There are a few sources, however, on Florida Indian attitudes toward blacks. We learn from Fontaneda that in the 1560s there was at least one black captive among the Calusa Indians in southwest Florida, but we have no evidence that his treatment was any different from that of their other captives from Spanish shipwrecks. From 1613 we have an indication that Timucua chiefs in north Florida held black slaves and that the Spaniards were particularly concerned about Indian-black relations. According to a bilingual Spanish and Timucua confessional, one of the questions the priest

1. For some aspects of this matter, see William S. Willis, Jr., "Divide and Rule: Red, White, and Black in the Southeast," *Journal of Negro History* 48, no. 3 (1963):157–76; reprinted on pp. 99–115 of "Red, White, and Black: Symposium on Indians in the Old South," *Southern Anthropological Society Proceedings* no. 5, ed. Charles M. Hudson (Athens, Ga., 1971). Kenneth W. Porter has about 15 very useful papers dealing with the Seminole Negroes; see, for example, "The Negro Abraham," *Florida Historical Quarterly* 25 (1946):1–43; "Farewell to John Horse: An Episode of Seminole Negro Folk History," *Phylon* 8 (1947):265–73; and "Negroes and the Seminole War, 1817–1818," *Journal of Negro History* 36 (1951):249–80. On the period treated by TePaske, Porter published "Negroes on the Southern Frontier, 1670–1763," *Journal of Negro History* 33 (1948):53–78. A recent volume by Porter reprints (with new annotations and introductions) some of his most important papers on Negro-Indian relations: *The Negro on the American Frontier* (New York: Arno Press and the *New York Times*, 1971).

2. See Alan Dundes' ground-breaking paper on "African Tales among the North American Indians," *Southern Folklore Quarterly* 29 (1965):207–19. Some genetic studies do indicate, however, that there is not much Indian ancestry in the American black population—e.g., William S. Pollitzer et al., "Blood Types of the Cherokee Indians," *American Journal of Physical Anthropology* 29 (1962):33–43.

had to ask a chief was whether he had held a black female slave as a mistress.[3]

In 1743, the surviving mainland and Keys Indians who settled at the mouth of the Miami River customarily killed English castaways, were antagonistic to the French, and were decidedly not under Spanish control. They were angry over the visit of two Jesuits from Havana, and blamed Captain Lucas Gómez, who had taken advantage of their respect and friendship, for introducing the priests—"They say they like him because he is a mulatto [Spanish *pardo*]," reported one of the Jesuits. One of my favorite items of Floridiana is a rare book published in Boston in 1760 which is the first-person account of a man I presume to have been a slave in Marshfield, Massachusetts, who was sent by his master as a crewman on a voyage to the Bay of Honduras for a load of logwood. On its return the ship ran aground off Miami Beach in 1748. Indians came out in canoes and killed all thirteen whites aboard, but recognized the author's difference and spared him. As he says, "they were better to me then [*sic*] my Fears, and soon unbound me, but set a Guard over me every Night." Five weeks later a passing Spanish schooner took him to Havana, but only four days after he got there his Indian captors arrived, having sailed a canoe over from Miami, and claimed him as their prisoner. The governor of Cuba ransomed him for $10.00. He was kept in Cuba for years, but evidently was treated as an Englishman more than as a slave. He finally made his way to England and then back to Marshfield after an absence of thirteen years.[4]

3. David O. True, ed., *Memoir of Do. d'Escalante Fontaneda Respecting Florida* (Coral Gables: Glade House, 1945) (note the Spanish references to "un mulato," "un negro," and "[un] negro horro" on pp. 71, 72, 73, with English translations on pp. 31, 33, 34); Francisco Pareja, *Confessionario en lengua Castellana, y Timuquana* (Mexico: Emprenta de la Viuda de Diego Lopez Daualos, 1613), p. 185 (there is a photostat and a typed transcript with John R. Swanton's interlinear translation of the Timucua in the National Anthropological Archives, Smithsonian Institution, MSS. 2401, 2446). I am indebted to Jerald T. Milanich, University of Florida, for showing me these passages.

4. The Jesuit was Joseph Xavier Alaña, in an enclosure with Juan Francisco de Guemes y Horcasitas, Governor of Cuba, to the Crown, 28 Sept. 1743, 58–2–10/15 in Archivo General de Indias, Seville; photostat in Stetson Collection, P. K. Yonge Library of Florida History, University of Florida. The pamphlet of 14 pages, found by the late John M. Goggin, is *A Narrative of the Uncommon Sufferings and Surprizing Deliverance of Briton Hammon, A Negro Man, Servant to General Winslow, of Marshfield, in New-England. Who returned to Boston. Printed and sold by Green and Russell, in Queen-Street, 1760*; copies are in the Library of Congress and the American Antiquarian So-

Let me now comment on Dr. Tanner's paper. The latter part of the eighteenth century was an extremely important period of Creek history. The origins of the later Creek state lie here; the separate Creek towns were aboriginally independent, but they began drawing together at this time. At the same period the Seminoles originated as "runaways" (the meaning of "Seminole" in the Creek language), that is, as frontier Creek settlers in North Florida who refused to join the amalgamation taking place among the older towns to the north. What one might call the conversion of the Creeks from a nationality to a nation began in response to just the sort of external pressures and opportunities touched on by these two papers.[5]

As one examines the documents, especially those on diplomatic and military affairs, the Creeks look more and more like a mini-state. A law code was written in English in 1818, with later revisions.[6] After the Creeks were shipped west to Indian Territory, they organized the Creek Nation, West, on a republican model, and after the Civil War the reorganized Muscogee Nation in Indian Territory had a full republican governmental apparatus. When this was abolished by the federal government with Oklahoma statehood in 1907, the Creek elite who had held the power and filled the government positions merged into the non-Indian population, keeping their legal enrollment as Creeks but severing social and cultural relations with the Creek masses.[7] The state apparatus was removed, making visible beneath it a Creek folk society in the Cookson Hills that could be seen to be very Indian. This is the society that anthropologists have studied, finding that Creek culture, Creek language, and Creek social and religious organization have survived very strongly.[8]

---

ciety and the latter reprinted it in their Readex-Microprint edition of American imprints.

5. See my chapter "Creek into Seminole," in *North American Indians in Historical Perspective*, eds. Eleanor Burke Leacock and Nancy Oestreich Lurie (New York: Random House, 1971), pp. 92–128.

6. "Laws of the Creek Nation," ed. Antonio J. Waring, University of Georgia Libraries Miscellanea Publications no. 1 (Athens, 1960).

7. For a useful brief summary see the article "Creek," in *A Guide to the Indian Tribes of Oklahoma*, ed. Muriel H. Wright (Norman: University of Oklahoma Press, 1951). A more detailed treatment of the history of the Creek Nation is Angie Debo's *The Road to Disappearance* (Norman: University of Oklahoma Press, 1941).

8. The most important anthropological studies of Creek culture are by John

This leads one to wonder how the government persisted and to ponder the exact relation of the Creek elite to the Creek folk even as early as the eighteenth century, when the separation began. The documents are not very helpful, for they were written by outsiders who were mainly dealing with the elite or by members of that elite. But the attempt should still be made to see behind the documents, or read between their lines, bearing in mind the later evidence for the persistence of traditional Creek society and culture and for the separation between the leaders and the led.

Around the time of the American Revolution, the European and Indian societies that were interacting across the southern frontier were separated by much greater cultural differences than we are used to in European history, or in later American history, including later Indian-white relations in the region. It was a situation that favored the growth of a class of intermediaries or cultural brokers, of entrepreneurs to facilitate and exploit the interaction between the two societies. Many of these men were genetically as well as culturally intermediate; as the sons of Scotch and English trader fathers and Creek mothers, they could maintain double social affiliation since the Creeks emphasized matrilineal descent.

One could say that the prestige, power, and income of these men depended to some degree on fooling both sides. One wonders whether they have not also succeeded in fooling some of the historians who have examined the documents they generated. I agree with Dr. Tanner and with the general opinion that Alexander McGillivray was a very important and remarkable man, but I have long wondered how Indian in culture he really was, and how much he participated in ordinary Creek society.[9] He grew up in Creek

---

R. Swanton, particularly his "Early History of the Creek Indians and Their Neighbors," Bureau of American Ethnology Bulletin no. 73 (Washington, 1922); "Social Organization and Social Usages of the Indians of the Creek Confederacy" and "Religious Beliefs and Medical Practices of the Creek Indians," in 42d *Annual Report of the Bureau of American Ethnology* (Washington, 1928), pp. 23–672; and (for technology and economy) "The Indians of the Southeastern United States," Bureau of American Ethnology Bulletin no. 137 (Washington, 1946). For a discussion of the unrepresentative nature of the Creek republican government of the late nineteenth century, see Morris Edward Opler, "The Creek 'Town' and the Problem of Creek Indian Political Reorganization," in *Human Problems in Technological Change, A Casebook*, ed. Edward H. Spicer (New York: Russell Sage Foundation, 1952), pp. 165–80.

9. The standard account is John Walton Caughey's *McGillivray of the Creeks* (Norman: University of Oklahoma Press, 1938). It contains a good biography and a fine collection of McGillivray's correspondence and papers.

country and went to school in Charleston for only three years. This seems entirely insufficient exposure to the English language and customs to account for McGillivray's later writing style and his obvious familiarity with Euroamerican politics. If he had an Indian name—and every true Creek man had more than one—we have no record of it.[10] Not long ago I examined the original treaty the Creeks signed in New York in 1790, including the secret articles that gave McGillivray a commission as brigadier general at $1,200 a year. The list of signatures on this treaty is very interesting. Among the Creeks, only McGillivray could write: he signed boldly, with a grand rubric under his name. All the rest signed by making a mark, and they are all very uncertain and poorly drawn X's, that look as though the signers had never held pens before. This is a great contrast with the skilled X's and many full names signed to an important Iroquois treaty four years later.[11]

10. The standard sources say his name was HopoyLmí·kko, but I believe this to be an error. That name is well documented as belonging to a contemporary, and opponent, of McGillivray's, a man also known in English as "the Tulsa King" (Tulsa = Tallassee and various other spellings). The Creek name is often translated as "the good child king." McGillivray's tribal town, Hickory-ground, was also known as Little Tulsa since it was an offshoot of Tulsa proper. An adult man's name, such as HopoyLmí·kko, was not supposed to be held by more than one living person in a given town. Such titles were also associated with specific clans, and Swanton has stated ("Social Organization," pp. 324, 326; cf. pp. 100–101) that as a Wind clansman at Hickory-ground, McGillivray was not entitled to bear a name ending with mí·kko ("chief" or "king"). The sole primary source on McGillivray's name seems to be John Pope's *A Tour Through the Southern and Western Territories of the United States of North-America; the Spanish Dominions on the River Mississippi, and the Floridas; the countries of the Creek Nation; and many Uninhabited Parts* (Richmond: John Dixon, 1792). Pope visited McGillivray at Little Tulsa and described his establishment and hospitality with admiration and gratitude. He gives the name only as one entry in a short Creek vocabulary (p. 65) taken down from Little King of Broken-arrow (another Creek tribal town) some days after he left McGillivray. The entry reads "Hippo ilk Micco, M'Gillivray, or the good child King." Evidently Little King dictated the Creek name (which was badly but recognizably spelled by Pope), and the "linguist" (interpreter) with them then explained that this was the name of "the Tulsa King" and could be translated "the good child King." Pope thereupon jumped to the wrong conclusion that by "the Tulsa King" was meant McGillivray, whom he knew as the most prominent man of Tulsa.

11. The Treaty of New York, 1790, and the Treaty of Canandaigua, 1794, both in the National Archives, Washington. It is possible that the Iroquois signers merely touched the pen used by a literate signer, as John C. Ewers tells me was the practice at some nineteenth-century treaty signings by Plains Indians. Nevertheless, the higher proportion of Iroquois able to write their own names remains notable.

McGillivray's career and personality deserve fresh study. It would also be instructive to look at three of his contemporaries or near-contemporaries who tried to play similar roles in the Creek world. One of these was a success and can be classed with McGillivray as a statesman and one of the founders of the Creek Nation, the American Benjamin Hawkins, former congressman and senator, who arrived in the Creek country as an agent in 1796, three years after McGillivray's death, and stayed until he himself died twenty years later. He managed to be both a Creek leader and reformer of Creek government, and an agent of the United States government.[12]

In a similar category I would put two failures, who can thus be called adventurers or confidence men. One of these is William Augustus Bowles, a Tory from Maryland who spent about ten years among the Creeks and Seminoles on four widely separated occasions between 1778, when he deserted from his regiment at Pensacola, and 1803, when the Creeks finally turned him over to the Spaniards who imprisoned him in Havana. He had a very adventurous career, during which he rather successfully passed himself off in England and the Bahamas as "Director General of the State of Muscogee," a title of his own invention. But he was seen to be a scoundrel by McGillivray and by many since—although a recent biographer tends, wrongly I believe, to accept his claim to status among the Creeks while scouting his boasts about his connections in England.[13]

The fourth figure I refer to is the marvelous French liar Louis LeClerc Milford, who spent about ten years among the Creeks beginning in 1785 and who claimed to have married McGillivray's sister. McGillivray quite clearly made use of him, but after McGillivray's death, Milford had to leave and he returned to France. He published a memoir in 1802 that no historian would take seriously but that, curiously enough, is used by anthropologists because it contains—incidentally to Milford's main promotional aims —data on Creek culture that later sources often confirm.[14]

12. Merritt B. Pound, *Benjamin Hawkins—Indian Agent* (Athens: University of Georgia Press, 1951).

13. J. Leitch Wright, Jr., *William Augustus Bowles, Director General of the Creek Nation* (Athens: University of Georgia Press, 1967).

14. Louis LeClerc de Milford, *Memoir or a cursory glance at my different travels & my sojourn in the Creek Nation*, trans. Geraldine de Courcy, ed. John

It seems clear that the late-eighteenth-century frontiers of the Creeks in Florida and Georgia deserve more attention from historians and anthropologists. It would be an appropriate Bicentennial celebration of this frontier to do a combined and comparative study of McGillivray, Hawkins, Milford, and Bowles, and their relations to the real Creek and Seminole people.

Francis McDermott (Chicago: The Lakeside Press, 1956). The editor also wrote an excellent historical introduction.

The Unique and the Universal in the History
of New World Colonization

MICHAEL G. KAMMEN

FINDING myself at a symposium on "Eighteenth-Century Florida and Its Borderlands," I feel very sympathetic to a poor, wayfaring bookplate of my acquaintance. Once when I was a graduate student browsing in the stacks of the Widener Library, I came across a book by Trevor R. Reese, *Colonial Georgia: A Study in British Imperial Policy in the Eighteenth Century* (1963). I was intrigued by its bookplate which read: "From the Fund Given by the Class of 1877 for the Purchase of Books on International Relations, Especially of the Far East." Now I know just how that bookplate must feel: happy to be in such good company, situated comfortably, but rather anomalous and out of place all the same. For I really know very little about either eighteenth-century Florida *or* its borderlands.

Given these problems, it seems necessary, if not the better part of valor, that I offer remarks whose texture and intent would be a little different from the other papers. It seems an occasion when I might be allowed to pursue questions rather than provide answers, and an opportunity to plunge into a broad subject in the manner once described by the late Carl Becker: "without scruple, without fear also, without reproach I hope, and certainly without research."[1]

What then is my subject, and what has led me to it? It is the phenomenon of colonization as a historical process, and I have come to it out of concern with the overwhelming particularity (and rela-

1. Becker to Frederick Jackson Turner, Turner Papers, Henry E. Huntington Library, San Marino, California.

tive parochialism) of most writings on the history of colonization. By writing colonial history within a national framework and from a monocultural perspective, historians have tended—implicitly or explicitly—to stress the unique rather than the universal, the narrative rather than the comparative approach. Certainly we must have the narrative before we can possibly have the comparative, and I think that an inventory of the unique and the particular is ultimately the indispensable stuff of history. But, having recently completed a book about the colonial origins of American civilization in which I too am primarily concerned with the specific sources of our indigenous culture,[2] I feel personally compelled to go back in time to the sector where the comparative (and the comparable), the universe (and the universal) await Clio's serious notice.[3]

If my subject may be defined as the common denominators of colonization, my purpose may be stated in words borrowed directly from Professor Lyle McAlister's remarkable essay on "Social Structure and Social Change in New Spain"—to use "a conceptual framework somewhat different from those commonly employed and one which may be more useful for the explanation of certain historical phenomena. . . . The principal concepts employed are abstracted from infinitely complex historical situations. A number of observations made cannot be documented precisely; they are hypotheses which seem to 'make sense' in the light of the author's reading and research. Hypotheses and substantiated observations, however, appear to fit together and to accommodate the known 'facts.' "[4]

Perhaps a celebration of the American Revolution Bicentennial in Florida is, after all, an appropriate occasion for these remarks; perhaps Florida was unique among the North American colonies in the eighteenth century precisely because of its universality. Florida had been colonized by the Spanish, the French, and the English. Moreover, those imperial powers recruited their colonists from a still broader range of sources: for example, 1,500 Corsicans, Greeks, Italians, and Minorcans were brought to New Smyrna in 1768. Throughout the sixteenth, seventeenth, and eighteenth centuries, Florida was being settled repeatedly, albeit sporadically and

2. *People of Paradox. An Inquiry into the Origins of American Civilization* (New York, 1972).

3. In a bibliographical appendix I have indicated some of the more interesting and valuable contributions to the comparative history of colonization. What is perhaps most striking is the relative paucity of such literature.

4. *The Hispanic American Historical Review* 43 (1963):349.

not always wisely or well. Florida as a paradise, Florida as a place of exploitation, Florida as an international pawn—the process was repeated over and over again, and it is precisely the matter of process, *of colonization as a process,* that I want to deal with here.

In order to do so, I think that one must look at the long history of human colonization: to the Mediterranean in antiquity, to the Orient, to northern Europe and the Levant during the Middle Ages, and, finally, to the sprawling epoch of European colonization in early modern times. The relevant literature is so vast that one might eventually filter out abundant evidence to support almost any hypothesis. If the English scheme in 1640 to place plantations in the Tapoywasooze and the Towyse–yarrowes countries on the coast of Guiana seems wildly unique, then the arrivals of Madoc, Ponce de León, and Adam Clayton Powell in Bimini over the centuries may symbolize certain recurring tendencies in the history of colonization. Neither of these whimsical illustrations proves a thing, of course, but a considered examination of the phenomenon of colonization seems to suggest generalizations of potential value.

Each phase in the history of colonial expansion has had its special hallmark or peculiar consequence. Through colonization the Greeks hellenized the ancient Mediterranean world, and the Romans militarized it. The Norse colonization of Iceland, Greenland, and Vinland was facilitated by their navigational skills. Norman expansion was made possible by their genius at political organization and assimilation. The Spanish colonized by the cross and conquest; the Italians and Dutch by commerce; the Portuguese by spices, avarice, and sexual aggressions; the French by fishing and fur-trading. But these are stylistic characteristics and stimuli, not the process itself. When historians look at the morphology common to all overseas expansion, they may find a certain similarity among the patterns. These four rubrics could prove useful for schematization: causes and sources of colonization; types of colonies and their common denominators; relations of colonizers with native peoples; and relations with the mother country.

As for causes and sources, successful colonization has usually occurred at a time of national consolidation (following the unification of Spain in 1479, for example, or Britain in 1603) and relative tranquility in international relations, linked with internal mobility or unrest. The colonizing country needs economic resources (sponsoring organizations or individuals), technical knowledge (modes of travel, geography, and construction), and charismatic leadership (the Greek *battus*). Very often there has been a socially pervasive *wandertrieb*, the urge to see over the horizon so characteristic of Thorfinn Karlsefni, Columbus, and Vasco da Gama. Commonly this urge has been stimulated by overpopulation at home (or the *belief* that overcrowding had set in), land hunger, a missionary impulse, and a desire for improved social position, mineral wealth, exotic products, or trade opportunities.

Militarism has often been a cause of colonization (and a consequence of it, as well). One need only look to the Hellenistic, Roman, Chinese, Norman, and Spanish experiences. Yet the initial military purposes and characteristics of colonies are rapidly transformed when professional soldiers find their self-defined roles incompatible with agricultural labor, and so refuse to work.

As the problem of culture and national identity gradually becomes acute in colonial dependencies, there is a common need to redefine one's role and the society's cosmology. Political power and leadership become functions of wealth rather than birth; neofeudal forms of social organization often appear; quarrels begin between ecclesiastical and secular authorities, between religious orders and other social groups. Even so, the process of colonization commonly tends to level society, blurring traditional distinctions and the extreme circumstances of high and low status. Nevertheless, many routine forms and styles of "home" life are often initially preserved, as architecture, food, and clothing, even where doing so is inappropriate or unnecessary.

Water has usually been a barrier to colonization until some conceptual or constructional revolution occurs; then the same body of water becomes a major thoroughfare for settling and provisioning new colonies. The choice of location has normally determined whether the venture could survive its inception. Colonies placed along trade routes have usually prospered; where the local trades and trade winds have been peculiarly seasonal, periods of intense activity have alternated with "dead times" of enforced leisure. The most successful colonizing ventures have been established in temperate or subtropical areas. Extremes of heat and cold, as in central Africa and Greenland, have produced rather different, more lethargic results.

Often colonization has led to the artificial creation or rebuilding of towns, especially towns designed as frontier spearheads. Normally there have been "land undertakers," as in medieval Germany and early modern Ireland, to promote and facilitate settlement, or some comparable device for the orderly distribution of land and lots. The systems of land allotment have frequently tended to create or accentuate new economic and social elites, and they, in turn, have subsequently shaped the colony's political culture.

In colonies which develop and mature quickly, utopian schemes either die an early death or are transformed. A crisis over the proper balance between authority and liberty often happens early. This crisis may involve controversies over citizenship, extraterritorial rights, or the structure of government. Local governance is of the greatest importance in early stages of colonial development, and is often perplexed by societal factors beyond its control, such as unanticipated geographic and social mobility or the premature desire for economic self-sufficiency.

My third common denominator of colonization encompasses the relationship between colonials and indigenous peoples. Despite encouragement from high officials to intermarry and have large families, relations have usually been difficult, marred by social, religious, or legal prejudice, and often by the colonizers' need for a well-organized and disciplined labor force. In race relations, the kinds of natives encountered—their customs, outlook, and level of development—are frequently as important and determinative as the policies of the newcomers.

There is a tendency to colonize areas of "inferior" cultural achievement; this not only re-inforces the settlers' sense of superiority, but causes them initially to idealize their original culture in its home setting. The indigenous peoples usually accept details, especially material advantages, but reject the colonizing culture as an integrated totality. Invariably certain economic and administrative functions elicit the emergence of a lonely go-between, be it the Portuguese *paulista*, the Russian *voevod*, or the French *coureur de bois*. There is the tendency of colonized areas eventually to become colonizers themselves: Normandy, England, the United States.

Fourth, relationships between colony and mother state are infinitely complex, as Plato observed in *The Laws* and Machiavelli noted so carefully in *The Prince*.[5] Contradictory aspirations among the various sponsors of colonization often interfere with the process

5. *The Laws,* paras. 735–36; *The Prince* (New York: Mentor ed., 1952), pp. 40–43.

itself, as in Portuguese Brazil and Jacobean Virginia. Where there is a conflict between generations at home, it is aggravated by transplantation to a new place where nationality becomes ambivalent or, worse yet, obscure. Many failures have occurred in the face of a hostile environment because of the lack of proper support from home (Greenland and Roanoke), or sheer ignorance of conditions in the place to be colonized.

Colonies have usually been politically subordinate, but the degree of their dependence has been lessened by distance, which impedes effective imperial administration. Colonial government and politics have commonly been affected by and tied to politics at home, in ways that were unhealthy for both but were inevitable. Nonetheless, provincial societies have not normally been microcosms of the mother country. Crucial social elements and groups are missing or much reduced in the scene overseas, causing strange sorts of imbalance, unexpected mobility, and inapplicable assumptions about "Politick Society." There is friction between established first-comers and late-comers. And, finally, the reasons men choose to stay are not always the same reasons that prompted them to come in the first place.

If we focus our attention on European expansion in the sixteenth, seventeenth, and eighteenth centuries, when Spain and England first planted their American outposts, the fundamental and specifically shared experiences become even more apparent. After the end of the fifteenth century, international contacts among peoples increased rapidly, and helped to produce a single, integrated world market. "Faced with new tasks," as E. L. J. Coornaert has commented, "the European peoples who bordered on the Atlantic developed and applied new economic techniques. They changed the framework of their economic organization, created new methods of cooperative action and new state departments and above all new merchant companies. They improved their techniques and their methods of using capital, changing their methods by a new organization of property and by a reintroduction of slavery. The states intervened more directly in economic affairs and slowly created modern colonies; their methods, in general terms, became accepted as *Mercantilism* and eventually developed into modern capitalism."[6]

6. "European Economic Institutions in the New World; the Chartered Companies," in *The Cambridge Economic History of Europe*, eds. E. E. Rich and C. H. Wilson (Cambridge, England, 1967), 4:220.

In almost every case, colonization occurred as states and men—but rarely statesmen—sought wealth from precious metals and trade. Few dreamed at the outset of creating colonial empires. Insofar as political motives moved the Renaissance princes, colonization was ancillary to a movement for strengthening and reorganizing their internal government and administration. Monopolies and national systems of exclusive trade might further those aims, of course, so colonies became doubly desirable. To a remarkable degree, each colony passed through stages of economic growth which led it "in the direction of the social conditions of its motherland."[7]

The social dimensions of colonization also provide us with striking sets of common denominators. That Cortez in 1502 and Raleigh in 1583 were prevented from sailing by the wiles of older women is true, but trivial. I am thinking, rather, of the roles played by younger sons of Europe's lesser nobility: by fidalgos, hidalgos, and the English gentry. I am thinking of the social conflict between Creoles and Peninsulares in New Spain, between mesticos and Portuguese in India, and between the South African–born and European-born in eighteenth-century Dutch South Africa. Similar distinctions and tensions were at the heart of social and political factionalism in the English North American colonies. The resentment directed by colonists against imperial inspectors provides yet another repetitive theme, as Louis Gaudais-Dupont, Edward Randolph, and José de Gálvez all discovered in various sectors of the Americas.

Finally, there was the ubiquitous connection (and strain) between social values and economic growth in the colonization experience. Because labor discipline was so important at the initial stages of settlement, institutions were devised to guarantee production, order, and stability. They attached each person to his role by providing incentives to insure his docility and sanctions to prevent his disobedience. Both the English and the French colonizers in North America were obliged somehow to recruit a labor force. The concessions they offered made it impossible to reproduce in the New World the clearly articulated, hierarchical social structure characteristic of contemporary Europe. The result was a familiar

7. Ibid., pp. 226, 228, 235; see also Achille Loria, "The Historical Revelation of the Colonies," translated, in *Turner and Beard: American Historical Writing Reconsidered,* ed. Lee Benson (New York, 1960), pp. 36–37.

pattern of upheaval in the seventeenth- and eighteenth-century colonies as traditional forms of social organization acquired some new equilibrium. Thus the distinct possibility of desirable social mobility—acquiring the wealth and status that gave one some claim to public regard—came as a consequence of the colonizing origins of North American societies: the peopling of those societies through the devices needed to recruit a voluntary labor force. The resulting social ideology that developed alongside these changes in social structure was one in which both public esteem and self-respect were largely dependent upon occupational success.[8]

I hope I am not so naïve as to attempt to reduce all the many dimensions of historical colonization to their common bases. In doing so, I would be no wiser than Tobias Hume, a Jacobean balladeer, who sang plaintively in 1605:

> Love makes men sayle from shore to shore
>   So doth Tobacco.
> Tis fond love often makes men poor,
>   So doth Tobacco,
> Love makes men scorne al Coward Feares,
>   So doth Tobacco.

My point is simply that there may very well be too few aspects of English or Spanish colonization, considered as an initial process, unique enough to enable us to locate the origins of our American civilization in that process per se. Are there even enough unique aspects, taken together as a configuration, to explain our cultural origins exclusively? I wonder. Three factors—one political, one economic, and one social—are often cited, but when examined closely and in comparative perspective, they do not support the argument with which they have been burdened.

The first of these claims is that the English Crown, unlike Castilian Spain for example, did not actively participate in and contribute to the colonization process until the third and fourth generation, when patterns of colonial autonomy had already been established. Now there is indeed a certain charm in finding Henry Wriothesley, Earl of Southampton and Shakespeare's patron, heading up a syndicate to send ships to America in 1602, helping later to run the Virginia Company, and dispatching Henry Hudson in

8. See Sigmund Diamond, "Values as an Obstacle to Economic Growth: The American Colonies," *Journal of Economic History* 27 (1967):561–75.

1610. But the colonization of southeast Asia by India in antiquity, most of the medieval Norse ventures, many of the later Dutch and some of the French schemes also took place without official governmental support, and in some cases actually in the face of official opposition!

A second claim has been that English colonization alone was peculiarly facilitated by new forms of economic organization, new ways of recruiting and utilizing capital. Again, the most superficial glance at the continental history of economic enterprise will disabuse us of this distortion, *except* to note and admit that the English experience with chartered companies was of unusually long standing and had medieval precedents.[9]

Finally, when we confront the traditional claim that English colonization was effected by whole families and communities—rather than by soldiers, trappers, and other celibate types—we are forced to look elsewhere to a long history of colonization by families and communities, beginning with the ancient Greeks. We must even acknowledge the indignant modern Hispanists, who insist that family transportation is one of the neglected aspects of Latin American colonial history.[10]

English colonization in the seventeenth and eighteenth centuries took place within the context of geographic and demographic assumptions common to the age and was facilitated by the expansion of capitalism in western Europe as well as by the opportunities offered by new investment patterns. The motives underlying English expansion were equally widespread: the quest for riches, converted souls, political dominion, and cultural expansion in a widening world. The assumption that the Indies would be reached by sailing westward, the common mercantile presuppositions, and the use of colonies to be rid of undesirable social elements at home all revealed England's proper place in the general expansion of Late Renaissance Europe. There were English proprietary grants, just as there had been *donatarios* in Brazil, *prazos* in West Africa, and feudal grants to Norman nobles in England by William the Conqueror. There were elaborate promotional campaigns accompanying

9. See Coornaert, "European Economic Institutions in the New World," pp. 222, 224, 236, 245.

10. James Lockhart, *Spanish Peru, 1532–1560: A Colonial Society* (Madison, 1968), chap. 9; Charles C. Griffin, "Unity and Variety in American History," in *Do the Americas Have a Common History? A Critique of the Bolton Theory,* ed. Lewis Hanke (New York, 1964), p. 256.

English colonization, as well as naïveté and outright stupidity concerning the heathen Indians' hopes and fears. And there were dissenters in the vanguard, English Brownists and Puritans, just as there had been French Huguenots in Florida and elsewhere.

Is it any wonder that Englishmen thought about colonization in generic and historic terms?[11] Medieval precedents, such as the Italian *fondaco* in the Levant, medieval measures for governing dependencies, and England's sixteenth-century experience with those wild folk across the Irish Sea, had all conditioned many men of the Stuart century to view their own ventures in the largest perspectives of time and space.[12] Thus, in 1681, William Penn generalized expansively in writing a tract for his own fledgling proprietary: ". . . there are [still] another sort of persons, not only fit for, but necessary in *plantations*, and that is, *men of universal spirits*, that have an eye to the good of posterity, and that both understand and delight to promote good discipline and just government among a plain and well intending people; such persons may find *room in colonies for their good counsel and contrivance*, who are shut out from being of much use or service to great nations under settl'd customs: these men deserve much esteem, and would be hearken'd to. Doubtless 'twas this . . . that put some of the famous *Greeks* and *Romans* upon transplanting and regulating *colonies* of people in divers parts of the world; whose names, for giving so great proof of their wisdom, virtue, labour and constancy, are with justice honourably delivered down by story to the praise of our own times."[13]

The story of English colonial consciousness of the history of colonization, and especially the immediate impact of that awareness

11. See Daniel Price, *Saules Prohibition Staide . . . Preached in a Sermon . . . the 28th of May, 1609* (London, 1609), reprinted in *The Genesis of the United States,* ed. Alexander Brown (Boston, 1890), 1:313 ff.; Sir Francis Bacon, "Of Plantations," in *The Works of Francis Bacon,* eds. James Spedding et al. (London, 1870), 6:457–59; Mildred Campbell, " 'Of People either too Few or too Many.' The Conflict of Opinion on Population and Its Relations to Emigration," in *Conflict in Stuart England: Essays in Honour of Wallace Notestein,* eds. W. A. Aiken and B. D. Henning (London, 1960), pp. 183–84.

12. See Howard Mumford Jones, "Origins of the Colonial Idea," in *Ideas in America* (Cambridge, Mass., 1945), pp. 48 ff.; Frederick Madden, "Some Origins and Purposes in the Formation of British Colonial Government," in *Essays in Imperial Government Presented to Margery Perham* (Oxford, 1963), pp. 6–8.

13. "Some Account of the Province of Pennsylvania," in *The Register of Pennsylvania,* ed. Samuel Hazard (Philadelphia, 1828–36), 1:308.

upon American Revolutionary thought, is a complex story which I have attempted to relate elsewhere.[14]

The particular experiences of various nations and groups in colonizing the New World are of vast importance for an appreciation of the causes of the American Revolution and for an understanding of our contemporary Third World. Taken singly, those experiences have not been neglected by historians and will not be in the future. But the similarities and attendant generalities ought not to be overlooked in the shuffle of note cards and national research.

This seems especially important in the case of colonial Florida because it underwent overlapping configurations of colonial conditions. I shall leave the possible applications and specifications to the Florida specialists. But I cannot help wondering whether colonial Florida's uniqueness rests paradoxically in its own universality. Wanted and unwanted, eagerly sought yet casually bargained away, a lush playground become a fortified battleground, Spanish and English, Catholic and Protestant, sheltered yet vulnerable—Florida would be many things to many men.

Floridians rejected revolutionary recourse in 1776, yet the reality and success of the American Revolution made the cession and absorption of Florida by the United States inevitable. According to traditional whiggish criteria of relevance, Florida was "irrelevant" to the coming of the American Revolution. In reality, however, Florida epitomizes the neglected side of the revolutionary experience, the Royalist side. Without understanding the Royalists, we cannot hope to understand the Whigs. It is more important for our purposes here, though, that the roots of Florida's royalism in 1776 —as well as her affiliative tendencies a generation later—lay in the original nature of Spanish and English colonization and their respective imperial policies.

Eighteenth-century Florida underwent phases of ambiguous constitutional and political legitimacy; it endured the precarious consequences of diplomatic instability, and its society was polyglot and pluralistic. In all these respects it was "American" even before it properly joined the United States in 1821. Having been colonized and controlled by several powers, its eventual identity would be

14. Kammen, ed., *The History of the Province of New York by William Smith, Jr.* (Cambridge, Mass., 1972), 1:xxxviii–lvi; Kammen, "The Meaning of Colonization in American Revolutionary Thought," *Journal of the History of Ideas* 31 (1970):337–58.

hybridized. All of which brings me back, once again, to my point of departure: that specificity may sometimes inhere in catholicity, and uniqueness derive from universality.

The literature on specific aspects of colonization, or concerning colonization by particular nations, is vast and very much in need of compilation into a bibliographical compendium. Although that task is inappropriate and impossible here, it might at least be useful to draw together some of the works which touch upon the comparative history of colonization and which would therefore be valuable as foundations for a more fully developed phenomenology than I have been able to offer. I have concentrated here upon colonization from antiquity until the eighteenth century. Modern colonization (since the 1780s) raises additional problems and requires other considerations and categories, such as colonization for purposes of social or political punishment.

Three of the earliest works are concerned with the colonial expansion of England and the United States during the second half of the nineteenth century: Herman Merivale, *Lectures on Colonization and Colonies* (London, 1861); Henry C. Morris, *The History of Colonization from the Earliest Times to the Present Day* (New York, 1900), 2 vols.; and Albert G. Keller, *Colonization: A Study of the Founding of New Societies* (Boston, 1908).

Herbert E. Bolton stressed themes common to both of the Americas in *The Colonization of North America, 1492–1783* (New York, 1920) and in "The Epic of Greater America," *American Historical Review* 38 (1933):448–74. The same sort of synthesis has been attempted more recently by a distinguished Latin Americanist, Silvio Zavala, in "A General View of the Colonial History of the New World," ibid. 66 (1961):913–29, and *The Colonial Period in the History of the New World* (Mexico, D.F., 1962).

Hispanists have provided us with some of our most valuable comparative insights. See Vera Rubin, *Plantation Systems of the New World* (Washington, 1959); Richard M. Morse, "Latin American Cities: Aspects of Function and Structure," *Comparative Studies in Society and History* 4 (1962):473–93; E. S. Urbanski, "Tradition and Mobility in Anglo-American and Spanish-American Civilizations: An Essay in Comparative History," *Cahiers D'Histoire Mon-*

diale 7 (1963):875–89; and a useful anthology edited by John J. TePaske, *Three American Empires* (New York, 1967).

The intellectual impact of colonization is treated by Edmundo O'Gorman, *The Invention of America* (Bloomington, 1961); Howard M. Jones, "Origins of the Colonial Idea," in *Ideas in America* (Cambridge, 1944), pp. 45–69; Kenneth S. Latourette, "Colonialism and Missions: Progressive Separation," *A Journal of Church and State* 7 (1965):330–49.

Over the past two decades French writers have been more willing than most to venture large generalizations about the phasing and phenomenology of colonization. See René Maunier, *The Sociology of Colonies* (London, 1949), 2 vols.; René Sedillot, *Histoire des Colonisations* (Paris, 1958); Frédéric Mauro, *L'Expansion Européene, 1600–1870* (Paris, 1964); and Pierre Chaunu, *Conquête et Exploitation des Nouveaux Mondes (XVIe Siècle)* (Paris, 1969). See also two books by the Belgian scholar Charles Verlinden: *Les Origines de la Civilisation Atlantique de la Renaissance à l'âge des Lumières* (Paris, 1966), and *The Beginnings of Modern Colonization* (Ithaca, 1970); and the first volume of *Südund Mittelamerika* by Richard Konetzke, subtitled *Die Indianerkulturen Altamerikas und die Spanisch-Portugiesische Kolonialherrschaft* (Frankfurt, 1965).

The potential impact of the social sciences upon the historiography of colonization may be seen by comparing three publications dated 1950, 1958, and 1961, with two others dated 1961 and 1964. See Merrill Jensen and R. L. Reynolds, "European Colonial Experience: A Plea for Comparative Studies," in *Studi in Onore di Gino Luzzatto* (Milan, 1950), 4:75–90; Ronald Syme, *Colonial Elites: Rome, Spain, and the Americas* (London, 1958); "Colonialism and Colonization in World History," a special issue of *The Journal of Economic History* 21 (1961); F. Mauro, "Towards an 'Intercontinental Model': European Overseas Expansion between 1500 and 1800," *Economic History Review*, ser. 2, 14 (1961):1–17; and Louis Hartz et al., *The Founding of New Societies* (New York, 1964).

British West Florida: Stepchild
of Diplomacy

ROBERT R. REA

THE modest claims of British West Florida to a place in the diplomatic history of the American Revolutionary Era were lost in the
clash of European empires and the turbulent struggle of the colonies for independence. Content to note West Florida's acquisition
in exchange for Cuba, historians initiate their accounts with the
Proclamation of 1763 which gave the colony institutional existence.
Its history ends with the Spanish seizure of Pensacola and the surrender of a conquered province in the Treaty of 1783. Recently, its
most distinguished chronicler has noted that the diplomatic history
of British West Florida merits closer study, and the subject has engaged the latest narrator of Anglo-Spanish rivalry in the New
World.[1] The extensive research of British and American diplomatic
historians will provide guidance for an exploratory essay on the
means by which West Florida was joined to and then parted from
the British empire, but the West Florida historian must also investigate unknown areas.

The initial problem is definition; West Florida should be seen as
the long coast embracing the Gulf of Mexico from the Bay of Espiritu Santo to the Balize. Though lacking any commonly accepted
continental boundaries, it was a necessary adjunct to every North
American empire, a magnet attracting the attention of all the Atlantic imperialists. Passed from France and Spain to England, it

1. Cecil Johnson, "West Florida Revisited," *Journal of Mississippi History*
28 (1966); J. Leitch Wright, *Anglo-Spanish Rivalry in North America* (Athens,
Ga., 1971).

was snatched back by Spain, then taken and absorbed by the United States. Such a history must be international—West Florida was the stepchild of diplomacy.

At the outset of the Great War for Empire in 1756, Spain held the Florida coast from the Castillo de San Marcos at St. Augustine to Pensacola's cedar-post stockade. French Mobile and New Orleans lay beyond. Carolinians and Georgians had long looked with fear and envy at the Spanish empire's northernmost redoubt and had dulled their swords and wasted their powder on its walls. Pensacola and Mobile were more distantly removed, but Anglo-American traders were familiar with those harbors. Where Charleston and Savannah businessmen sought profits, British entrepreneurs were also interested. British interest in the Gulf ports was essentially commercial. At Dauphin Island and Mobile, merchants found a welcome for those who carried the goods France could not provide, and during the Seven Years War, the French governor of Louisiana would defend illicit wartime commerce as necessary for the very existence of his colony. More than New Orleans, Mobile attracted the Anglo-Americans because of its proximity to the Indian country beyond the British frontier, and colonial governors looked enviously toward the Gulf of Mexico.[2]

In 1756, Governor Lyttelton of South Carolina proposed to send a large body of militia and Indians against Fort Condé at Mobile, supported by 1,000 British regulars with artillery. Mobile, once taken, might serve as a base for operations against New Orleans. Early in 1757, the governor of New York, hearing rumors of French troop movements north from New Orleans, urged William Pitt to launch an attack on the capital of Louisiana. In April he reiterated his plea and pointed out the desirability of establishing naval surveillance at the mouth of the Mississippi.

In January 1758, Pitt instructed Governor Lyttelton to transmit to Admiral Boscawen at Halifax whatever intelligence he could gather respecting "the forts on the rivers Mobile and Mississippi; the navigation of those two rivers; and the practicability of any attempt to be made, towards the latter end of the year, by a body of troops, that may be sent . . . by sea." At the same time Pitt directed that any pilots or seamen familiar with New Orleans should

2. N. M. Miller Surrey, *The Commerce of Louisiana during the French Regime, 1699–1763* (New York, 1916), pp. 444–63; *Account of the European Settlements in America* (London, 1758).

be dispatched to Halifax to provide Boscawen with further information. An attack upon both Mobile and New Orleans was envisaged, and Pitt urged the governor of South Carolina to plan a coordinated land campaign against Fort Toulouse in the Alabama country. However, the minister and his commanders had determined that Louisbourg and Quebec should be the primary targets of the next major British thrust; Mobile would become the focus of a southern expedition only if the season grew too late for action in the North. Governor Dobbs of North Carolina was ready to offer local support, and in 1759 he stressed to Pitt "the necessity . . . of driving the French from Mobile." That year, the *annus mirabilis* of Pitt's career, saw British power established at Quebec rather than at New Orleans, but with the fall of Canada, Anglo-American attention turned south in earnest. Dobbs wrote of Britain's "prior right" to the mid-Mississippi region and held that its annexation was "absolutely necessary for the peace and safety of these colonies." His view was supported at Charleston in March 1760 by Edmund Atkin, who had recently returned from negotiations with the tribes on the frontier. Atkin was optimistic about the success of a seaborne attack on Mobile, but felt that an overland venture from the Atlantic coastal colonies "would be powerfully opposed" by the Francophile Indians. Nonetheless, Atkin urged that "whenever a peace shall be made with France, the possession of the harbour of Mobile is absolutely necessary to the security of our southern colonies." Further pleas for action came from the lieutenant governor of Georgia, Henry Ellis, who called for a naval expedition against Mobile in conjunction with the seizure of the French frontier forts Toulouse and Tombecbé.

By October 1760 the British government was ready to launch a southward blow. General Amherst was warned to prepare for an attack upon either Louisiana or the West Indies, and at that moment Louisiana seemed the preferred objective. Amherst anticipated the dispatch of forces down the Mississippi River, by way of Detroit and the Maumee-Wabash route, and coordinated naval operations at the mouth of the river. His scheme entailed the most daring and extended military advance into Indian country ever proposed by the British army, but his dreams were ended in December, when Pitt's first choice was set aside by his ministerial colleagues' preference for easier and richer conquests in the Caribbean.

Throughout the war, in fact, neither French nor British military plans in the southwest passed beyond the stage of discussion. Each sought to utilize its Indian allies against the other, but neither possessed the resources with which to launch a full-scale campaign. This was especially true of the impoverished French at New Orleans, isolated as they were by the supremacy of the British navy. However, seapower did not interdict American colonial commerce. In 1760, Pitt urged the North American and West Indian governors to act against trade with the enemy at Mobile and New Orleans; but, as was to be expected, insufficient evidence was discovered by American officials to justify legal action which would run counter to American economic interests.[3]

Pitt's failure to press an attack upon the Gulf coast may be attributed to his grasp of overall strategy and the political necessity of maintaining harmony in the ministry after the death of George II and the accession of his grandson in October 1760. With the fall of Canada, the French in America were impotent, and their remaining properties might be had by negotiation more easily than by the sword. At home, George III brought into positions of power new men whom even Pitt did not dare to ignore. So, while the navy struck at the French sugar islands, Pitt concentrated on the diplomatic front. Early in 1761 he realized that France was preparing her move, to bring Spain into the war. While the Great Commoner considered the international balance and decided to outdo Spain, lesser men brought about his political demise. A frightened Duke of Newcastle and a nervous Earl of Bute combined to bring Pitt down in October 1761. The war would continue, even expand, but the government headed by Bute would seek peace—not without keeping an eye on the Gulf coast, Spanish Florida, and French Louisiana, mindful of Spanish complaints that Georgians were encouraging Indian disturbances around Pensacola.[4]

More than any other power, Spain could boast of a policy toward the Gulf coast—a policy of exclusion based upon her aged claim to universal dominion and her current fears of economic competition. In November 1759, Charles III of Spain had memorialized the Court of St. James to the effect "that he could not see with indiffer-

---

3. On the various Anglo-American projects, see Gertrude S. Kimball, ed., *Correspondence of William Pitt, When Secretary of State, with Colonial Governors and Military and Naval Commissioners in America* (New York, 1906).
4. *Papers Relative to the Rupture with Spain* (London, 1762), p. 37.

ence the considerable conquests of the English in America, and that if they did not make peace he would be compelled to make war."[5] As French Foreign Minister Choiseul was already expecting to lose Louisiana to the British, Spain's position in North America was hazardous at best. Ambassador Fuentes in London moaned, "Who shall stop their conquests, if the English make themselves masters of Martinico and attack [the] Mississippi. Today it will be at the expence [*sic*] of the French. Tomorrow at that of the Spaniards."[6] In fact, Spain's chief hope lay in falling heir to the leavings of France, an inheritance not incompatible with British interests in view of Spain's weakness.

In the summer of 1760, Charles III began to hint at a desire for French Louisiana. The next year Choiseul, desperate for aid, offered it as bait in exchange for Spain's entry into the war and financial assistance for the empty French treasury. Had the French minister pursued a straight course, he might have saved Louisiana —it had not been conquered, and Anglo-French negotiations were based upon the principle of *uti posseditis*—but Choiseul insisted upon involving Spain in the current negotiations and quibbled over the boundary of Canada. Anglo-French discussions were broken off in September 1761, and Pitt made the fatal demand for a preventive attack upon Spain which led to his ouster from the cabinet. Choiseul's plans matured slowly. Charles III procrastinated and refused to open hostilities against Britain until January 1762, when Britain tardily declared war on Spain and thereby activated the Bourbon alliance.[7]

With the outbreak of the Anglo-Spanish conflict, the British government began to implement its plans for the seizure of the Gulf coast. General Amherst was to be loosed upon New Orleans and the Earl of Albemarle upon Pensacola, after he had conquered Havana. Many thought a blow against the southern coast of North

5. Roger H. Soltau, *The Duke de Choiseul* (Oxford, 1909), p. 51.

6. Kate Hotblack, *Chatham's Colonial Policy* (London, 1917), pp. 131–32.

7. On the negotiations leading to the Peace of Paris, see Kate Hotblack, "The Peace of Paris, 1763," *Transactions of the Royal Historical Society*, 3d ser., 2 (1908); Zenab E. Rashed, *The Peace of Paris* (Liverpool, 1951); W. R. Shepherd, "The Cession of Louisiana to Spain," *Political Science Quarterly* 19 (1904); Arthur S. Aiton, "Diplomacy of the Louisiana Cession by France to Spain, 1763," *American Historical Review* 36 (1931); E. Wilson Lyon, *Louisiana in French Diplomacy 1759–1804* (Norman, Okla., 1934); Richard Pares, *War and Trade in the West Indies, 1739–1763* (Oxford, 1936); Max Savelle, *The Origins of American Diplomacy* (New York, 1967).

America was long overdue, and the people of England expected much from the Havana expedition. But even as Spain entered the war, Choiseul sought to extricate France by renewing peace negotiations. Bute's ministry was embarrassed by British successes, and, with the French West Indies at his disposal, the earl could demand even more in North America than Pitt had dared to ask. In May 1762, Secretary of State Egremont proposed that the Mississippi be adopted as the western boundary of British North America, a modest claim against the vastness of French Louisiana, and at first he demanded New Orleans, too. But for once Choiseul was fortunate. Bute's fatuous desire for peace—pursued through the more or less secret channels of the Sardinian ambassadors Viry and Solar—led him to adopt the Iberville-Pontchartrain line of demarcation, which excluded New Orleans from the proposed cession.[8] Choiseul promptly took up this unexpected advantage and acquiesced in the transfer of Mobile to Britain, leaving to Bute the awkward task of silencing Egremont and George Grenville who protested the surrender of British claims to New Orleans. It took Bute three weeks to convince his colleagues that he would insist upon free navigation of the river. Choiseul recognized that Spain might object to the arrangement, but, he declared, " 'We will make her listen to reason. If she takes it badly, we will propose to her the exchange of Florida . . . for whatever remains to us of Louisiana.' "[9]

Spain protested the prospect of English neighbors on the Gulf coast, and demanded written assurance that the Mobile region would not be ceded to Britain. But Choiseul, determined to have peace, was ready to betray his ally in order to salvage something in the West Indies. He guaranteed Mobile to England by a secret article unknown to Spain, and he advised Britain that if Spain balked at accepting the cession of Mobile, France would sign a peace treaty without her. Only by securing the Iberville-Pontchartrain boundary did Choiseul show the slightest regard for the interests of Spain.

By the end of July 1762, Bute felt that he could settle with France, but the fate of the Havana expedition was still undecided

8. Theodore Pease, "The Mississippi Boundary of 1763," *American Historical Review* 40 (1935):279–82. The Viry-Solar negotiation was not really very secret; Joseph Yorke at the Hague knew of it, as did the Dutch and Prussian ambassadors and "France generally." Philip C. Yorke, *The Life and Correspondence of Philip Yorke, Earl of Hardwicke* (Cambridge, 1913), 3:358.

9. Savelle, *Origins of American Diplomacy*, pp. 496–97.

and Bute's colleagues were anxious to pin down Spain along with France. The Duke of Bedford, about to depart as plenipotentiary to Versailles, insisted upon having specific instructions as to how far he should press the Spanish in the event of news of the taking of Havana. Bute "wished they could be brought to yield St. Augustine" and noted that "some wished for Porto Rico."[10] In August, public and politicians alike were waiting for word from Cuba, and journalists, presuming that Havana must already have fallen, warned that the public would not be satisfied with anything less than "so poor an equivalent" as Spanish Florida.[11] Bedford arrived in Paris to discover that Choiseul had not yet informed the Spaniards of the Anglo-French agreement regarding Mobile and still wished to keep it secret.

News of the fall of Havana reached London on September 29, 1762, and Bute faced a cabinet crisis. He did not dare approve a treaty that failed to secure adequate compensation for the restoration of Cuba to Spain. Florida was the most likely property for which to barter, but Grenville and Egremont were violent in their demands that both Florida and Puerto Rico must be acquired. About October 8, Bute decided to ask for Florida alone, and, to strengthen his hand, he brought Henry Fox and the Earl of Halifax into the ministry. By applying the most severe political pressure, Bute was able to secure cabinet agreement that Britain would accept either Puerto Rico or Florida as compensation for Cuba, but even Bute had to admit to his plenipotentiary that "Our demands are trivial compared with the important conquest we give up."[12]

As for Spain, the loss of Havana put an end to pride. Without Cuba, all else would be lost. Belatedly concerned for his partner's satisfaction, Choiseul offered to cede New Orleans and the western portion of French Louisiana to Britain in order to guarantee the restoration of Spanish colonies. But the French offer was rejected as less desirable to Britain than Florida, and the Spanish themselves could see little point in retaining Florida, surrounded as it would be by British territory. At this point, Louis XV magnani-

10. John Russell, ed., *Correspondence of John, Fourth Duke of Bedford* (London, 1842–46), 3:96.

11. *Political Controversy* (London, 1762), p. 332; *The Monitor,* September 25, 1762.

12. *Bedford Corr.,* 3:138. See also Nelson V. Russell, "The Reaction in England and America to the Capture of Havana, 1762," *Hispanic American Historical Review* 9 (1929).

mously offered western Louisiana to Spain, not for the waging of war, but for the easier digestion of an unpalatable peace. Having no prospect of holding Florida if he would recover Cuba, knowing at last that Britain would have Mobile in any case, Charles III agreed as graciously as possible to the French offer and the Anglo-French preliminaries. Signatures were affixed on November 3, 1762, accomplishing the transfer of Florida and eastern Louisiana from Spain and France to Great Britain and the remainder of Louisiana, along with New Orleans, from France to Spain.

Britain won the Gulf coast without launching a blow against its defenses, but only her unparalleled military success elsewhere in the Caribbean saved the Gulf ports from direct attack—that and the fevers which decimated Albemarle's army at Havana and made further campaigning almost impossible. Few Englishmen cheered the acquisition, however. As Charles Townshend told the King, Florida "was an uninhabited country and could not be look'd on as any . . . but a useless territory," to which His Majesty replied that "Florida from its fertility and goodness of climate was capable of the greatest improvement." Bute observed that when it was rumored that Spain had ceded Puerto Rico, "the cry then was for Florida . . . now the same mouths vomit out curses against Florida." At least one cartoonist then proceeded to roast the Scottish Earl on a fire stoked with "Florida Turf."[13]

Many would decry Bute and his peace, but the Floridas were British and the ambitions of colonial administrators and merchants were momentarily satisfied. The eastern continental limits of North America were neatly rounded off, but at a price—the key to the Caribbean and the Gulf of Mexico, which had been conquered, and the whole vast Mississippi basin west to the Rockies, which had been freely offered. Never had imperial Britain rejected such riches in order to retain so insignificant a prize. Nor had France and Spain displayed much desire to retain the Floridas. On both sides the Gulf coast colonies were viewed as pawns to be sacrificed, almost painlessly, to bring to an end that "bloody and expensive" war. British victories made a triumphant peace inevitable, but it was Bute's frantic pursuit of terms acceptable to his enemies,

13. Romney Sedgwick, ed., *Letters from George III to Lord Bute, 1756–1766* (London, 1939), p. 161; *Bedford Corr.*, 3:152; *British Museum Catalogue of Prints: Satires*, 4, no. 4045. See also Charles L. Mowat, "The First Campaign of Publicity for Florida," *Mississippi Valley Historical Review* 30 (1943).

Choiseul's readiness, in the face of financial disaster, to withdraw from North America altogether, and Spain's total ineptitude that determined the territorial results.

Britain's shield protected the West Florida coast through a dozen quiet years. Only when O'Reilly's troops enforced Spain's authority in New Orleans and the Falkland Islands crisis threatened the European peace did Pensacola and Mobile become internationally significant. Had war broken out in 1771, British troops might have struck at New Orleans with some expectation of success, but the crisis passed and a growing stream of settlers moved into the rich lands of Mississippi. West Florida was effectively isolated from the troubles that led the Atlantic colonies toward revolution, but once the Continental Congress had given voice to an American consciousness, the Floridas were borne into a new complex of warring national and international aspirations.[14]

In 1774, the Congress sought support at Pensacola and addressed a letter to the speaker of the provincial assembly, but the attorney general, into whose hands it fell, merely referred it to the royal governor. Pensacola had no revolutionary tocsin, but American nationalists—Benjamin Franklin among them—envisioned a colonial union which would include both the Floridas. In September 1776, an American agent appeared at New Orleans, talking of the seizure of Pensacola and inquiring if Spain was interested in its acquisition, which it was. Young Governor Bernardo de Gálvez saw to it that Spanish neutrality served the commercial interests of Oliver Pollock and, later, the filibustering endeavors of James Willing. For the moment, however, he was more concerned for the security of New Orleans than for the conquest of her neighbors, and he restricted himself to a cautious surveillance of the British colony.

Congress would go further. Eager to seize the prize, the Board of War, in July 1777, recommended that General Edward Hand and 1,000 men be sent down the Mississippi against Mobile and Pensacola. The timing of the proposal was unfortunate, though, and after

14. On the diplomacy of the American Revolution, see Samuel Flagg Bemis, *The Diplomacy of the American Revolution* (Bloomington, Ind., 1957); Richard W. Van Alstyne, *The Rising American Empire* (New York, 1960); Van Alstyne, *Empire and Independence* (New York, 1965); Richard B. Morris, *The Peacemakers* (New York, 1965); Gerald Stourzh, *Benjamin Franklin and American Foreign Policy* (Chicago, 1954); John J. Meng, *The Comte de Vergennes* (Washington, 1932); Vincent T. Harlow, *The Founding of the Second British Empire* (London, 1952); Piers Mackesy, *The War for America 1775–1783* (Cambridge, Mass., 1964).

considerable discussion and opposition on the ground that the effort would waste America's slim resources, the project died. For the United States, the first order of business was the establishment of alliances with France and Spain. Silas Deane and Benjamin Franklin approached Louis XVI's foreign minister, the Comte de Vergennes, in the winter of 1776–77 with a proposal whereby France would secure Britain's West Indian possessions and the United States secure the two Floridas. From Philadelphia came the suggestion that, in exchange for a Spanish alliance, the United States might assist in the conquest of Pensacola and allow it to revert to Spain if the free use of the harbor and free navigation of the Mississippi were assured to the Americans.

Increasing unofficial French and Spanish aid in 1777 moved the Bourbon powers closer to a break with Britain, and in January 1778 the Franco-American alliance was concluded—in terms which allowed for American absorption of all the British colonies in North America, including the Floridas. Both France and the United States were eager to secure active Spanish participation, and Vergennes' overtures to Madrid became increasingly tempting and specific. Professing no desire to see the United States "mistress of the entire continent," he insinuated that even if the United States took Florida by its own efforts, Pensacola should be given to Spain. It was a short step to a direct offer of Florida in return for a Spanish alliance. Conrad-Alexandre Gérard was sent to Philadelphia to make it clear to Congress that France was not enthusiastic about American expansion and that Spain had a prior claim on the Floridas. His Spanish counterpart, Juan de Miralles, won Gérard's full support for his government's view that Spain alone must be allowed to conquer and possess the Floridas, and the Bourbon allies achieved a rare unity of purpose vis-à-vis American ambitions along the Gulf coast. Gérard's influence was apparently effective, for the Foreign Affairs Committee instructed the Paris mission in October 1778 to seek a western boundary for the United States on the Mississippi River, but to ask for no more than free passage on its lower stretches and the use of one or more ports in Spanish territory.

Charles III acted with accustomed deliberation. Whereas in October 1778 the Spanish Minister Floridablanca expressed a vague willingness to see Florida pass to the United States, except that portion necessary to safeguard Gulf navigation, in November he

proposed to declare war against England only if Spain were assured a free hand to seize Florida. The government of Charles III
was determined to give no countenance and little comfort to rebel
colonists. At this early date Spain seems to have considered the
Americans as much enemies as were the British. In February 1779,
Vergennes assured Spain of the possession of Mobile and the restitu-
tion of Pensacola, but Floridablanca continued to procrastinate, and
in April he presented new demands for an alliance. In the initial exchanges, Spanish designs upon Gibraltar had occupied a secondary
place, but, having secured French assurances concerning the Gulf
coast, Floridablanca now put Gibraltar first on his list and, accepting the French proffer of West Florida, insisted upon East Florida
as well. Vergennes accepted his terms, and the Convention of Aran-
juez was concluded. The American Congress did its part by pledg-
ing supplies to Spain if she attacked the Floridas. On June 21, 1779,
Spain declared war on Britain. Her goal in America was the recovery of the Floridas. It was fully approved by Vergennes and supported in Philadelphia by his emissary; it was effectively accepted
by the United States Congress when, on August 14, 1779, it agreed
to the thirty-first parallel as the boundary for West Florida, part of
a package of peace terms.

The involvement of West Florida in Anglo-Spanish hostilities was
not unforeseen. When France entered the war in 1778, the West
Indies became an area of critical concern for Britain; orders were
issued for the reinforcement of the Gulf coast bases, and George
III appeared to be determined to hold the Floridas even if it became necessary to evacuate the rebellious thirteen colonies in order
to meet the French threat. An American filibustering expedition, led
by former West Floridian James Willing, attacked the British posts
on the Mississippi. Though unable to effect permanent occupation or
the displacement of British authority, Willing's raid demonstrated
the vulnerability of the colony's western sector.[15] In the fall of
1778, Bernardo de Gálvez proposed a joint Spanish-American attack upon Pensacola, but Congress was unable to act on his suggestion. The governor of Havana was instructed to seek an American contingent of 4,000 men for use against either St. Augustine or
West Florida, and the Spanish agent Miralles negotiated with the
Congress and General Washington for American military aid. At the

15. John Caughey, "Willing's Expedition down the Mississippi, 1778,"
Louisiana Historical Quarterly 15 (1932).

same time an American agent visited Havana, seeking to concert action against the British in Georgia and Florida, but he received no encouragement. On the other hand, as soon as Spain became a belligerent, British forces in West Florida were ordered to attack New Orleans, but local commander General John Campbell was not the man to seize the initiative. It was left to the impetuous Gálvez at New Orleans to act on his own proud motto—*Yo Solo!*—and unleash an attack upon Britain's inadequately defended Mississippi settlements. General Campbell frittered away his manpower and, between 1779 and 1781, lost the colony piecemeal.

With Spain at last engaged, the United States pressed yet more vigorously to secure an alliance. Congressional desire for the Floridas was apparent during debates on the instructions to be given the representative destined for Spain, but the painful disabilities of the American military and financial situations were overwhelming. Congress concluded that diplomatic recognition and a Spanish alliance were worth more than Florida. If Spain could conquer Florida, she might have it—assuming, of course, that the United States might enjoy free navigation of the Mississippi. With these instructions John Jay departed on a most frustrating diplomatic mission.

Floridablanca was fully determined to obtain West Florida and the Gulf coast. He advised the British agent Richard Cumberland of this in the spring of 1780, and Cumberland suggested that Britain might be persuaded to exchange West Florida for Puerto Rico. With little prospect of conquering East Florida, Spain was prepared to leave it in British hands in spite of Commodore George Johnstone's hint that it might be recovered if Spain would lend assistance against the United States.[16] John Jay could make no effective proposals of any sort. His offers of military support against Pensacola were laughable when combined with his pleas for Spanish subsidies. American fortunes were low, and the Spanish government was unwilling to cooperate in any way until its exclusive possession of the Gulf coast was assured. Early in 1781, Congress instructed its representative to surrender to Spain all claims upon the lower Mississippi and the Gulf coast in a final effort to gain recognition and support. In September, Jay accepted the inevitable and offered everything below the thirty-first parallel in exchange for an alliance.

16. Samuel Flagg Bemis, *The Hussey-Cumberland Mission* (Princeton, 1921), pp. 41, 49.

The military campaigns of 1781 proved decisive. Gálvez captured Pensacola for Spain, and Franco-American forces at Yorktown ended Britain's hope of victory on the North American continent. Lord North's government collapsed in March 1782, and his successors, Rockingham and Shelburne, had to make peace as best they could. The American diplomats concentrated on Paris, and Jay, bristling with distrust of Spain, added a critical element to their counsels.

In Paris, Spain was represented by the Conde de Aranda, with whom Jay discussed American ambitions with a degree of candor unknown at Madrid. Early in August 1782, their conversations turned to the western boundary, and Jay indicated that the United States would insist upon the Mississippi. Aranda observed that if the river line were accepted, Spain would lose West Florida. "Not only did that used to be ours," said Aranda, "but we have reconquered it from the English." Jay's argument that the United States was the rightful inheritor of Britain's claims elicited the retort that conquest carried higher rights which belonged to Spain. Aranda's determination to retain West Florida was further displayed when Vergennes proposed to establish the Hispano-American boundary on a line drawn north from Fort Toulouse, thereby assuring Spain of the Mississippi and Mobile, but not Pensacola. In spite of the considerable advantages of Vergennes' scheme, Aranda insisted that the remainder of West Florida must also be guaranteed to Spain. Later in the month, Jay's exchanges with the Spaniard became acidulous. When Aranda reminded him of the many Spanish efforts in behalf of the United States, the American accused Spain of selfishly grabbing Pensacola for herself and showing singular bad faith by allowing its garrison to go to New York where it was employed against American forces.[17]

In view of Spain's refusal to recognize the United States, to sign an alliance, or to agree to a boundary settlement satisfactory to the United States, and fearing that France would sacrifice the interests of the American ally for whom she had done so much in order to pacify the European ally for whom she had accomplished so little, Jay turned to the English who promised a more friendly reception. Both Shelburne and his agent in Paris, Richard Oswald, were desirous of retaining East Florida. Spurred on by Benjamin Vaughan,

17. Samuel Flagg Bemis, "The Rayneval Memoranda of 1782," in *American Foreign Policy and the Blessings of Liberty* (New Haven, 1962), pp. 49, 55, 58.

Oswald seems to have developed an idea which in October 1782 resulted in Jay suggesting that Britain should use the 20,000 troops remaining in North America to recover West Florida, at one step accomplishing both their removal from New York and the exclusion of the Spanish from the east bank of the Mississippi. The project so warmed Jay, reported Oswald, that he " 'came again upon the subject of West Florida & pled in favour of the future commerce of England as if he had been of her Council.' "[18] The other United States commissioners endorsed Jay's proposition. Franklin backed it enthusiastically, insisting only that Anglo-American collusion should not be disclosed by the employment of troops from New York for an attack upon Pensacola. Oswald then suggested that if the scheme were accomplished, the Anglo-American boundary of West Florida might be established on the thirty-fourth parallel. Jay was not prepared to discuss that technicality, but Oswald pursued the matter at home, noting that the United States was so hostile toward Spain that it might even attempt the seizure of West Florida for itself. Benjamin Vaughan supported Oswald with the observation that the recovery of West Florida would provide Britain with a refuge for displaced Loyalists as well as economic and commercial access to the American West. While Shelburne was sensitive to the cause of the Loyalists, he had apparently already lost all hope of retaining West Florida well before Jay's remarkable proposal was made. He told a French agent in September that Britain was not interested in the Gulf coast, though he might consider an exchange of Gibraltar for the restoration of all French and Spanish conquests (which would, of course, include West Florida) and additional compensation in the West Indies.

American and British negotiators approached agreement early in October when Jay produced a preliminary draft treaty which would set the United States southern boundary at 31°N. The boundary proposal was acceptable to Shelburne, but the idea of a British expedition to recover West Florida was far from attractive. Secretary of State Thomas Townshend rejected it because he feared that Gulf coast naval operations would expose Britain's West Indian holdings. He spoke of the project as an "absurdity" and feared it was a trick of the Allies. By late October, however, it was clear that Britain's enemies were anything but united. Reconsidering the proposition, Townshend advised Oswald that " 'The Colony of West

18. Harlow, *Founding of the Second British Empire*, 1:304–6.

Florida is certainly an object of our attention, and we should be extremely glad to adopt such measures as might ensure us the repossession of it.' "[19] A body of London merchants added their support to the idea of recovering West Florida, and Henry Strachey was instructed to sound out Jay as to the use of the British troops at New York for that purpose. Nothing came of it, for Strachey cooled the incipient Anglo-American entente by demanding restrictive American boundaries elsewhere. The thirty-first degree proposal remained negotiable, however, and as various possible arrangements were discussed, it became clear that the American commissioners would accept a more moderate settlement of their claims upon the territory, should West Florida ultimately revert to George III, than they would agree to if the colony remained with Spain. Jay's second draft treaty secretly provided that if Britain secured West Florida as a result of her negotiations with France and Spain, the Anglo-American boundary should be set at 32°28'N, the Yazoo River line which had been the northern boundary of British West Florida. In this form the Anglo-American preliminaries were signed in Paris on November 30, 1782. The next day Franklin notified Vergennes of all but the secret article relative to West Florida—and eased his conscience on the ground that the special circumstances that would make it effective had not yet developed.

In spite of the virtual reversal of alliances by the American diplomats, England's chances of recovering West Florida were slight. As she would not take to the field for its reconquest, she must win it at the conference table, and Anglo-Spanish diplomacy orbited around Gibraltar rather than Pensacola. Early in October, Vergennes tested Spain's desire for and Britain's dedication to Gibraltar by suggesting that, as Shelburne seemed willing to discuss its cession to Charles III, Spain should offer both Floridas, New Orleans, and any claims she might have on territory east of the Mississippi, thereby establishing a British buffer between the United States and the Spanish American empire to the west. This scheme —fascinating as it appears in retrospect—pleased no one. Britain had already decided to let the trans-Appalachian West go to the United States; the Americans had determined to reject anything less than a Mississippi River boundary; and even Floridablanca scoffed at the proposal, for he had no desire to see British traders ensconced along the Gulf coast. When Aranda opened negotiations

19. Ibid., p. 307; Morris, *Peacemakers*, p. 352.

with the British at Paris, he declared West Florida to be a *sine qua non*, but the Spaniard vacillated for a moment when he imagined that West Florida might serve as an equivalent for Gibraltar—a misconception attributable to Vergennes rather than to the British representative who had suggested only that British acquiescence in the loss of West Florida might be purchased by the return of Minorca or the Bahamas. When Floridablanca learned that the proposal involved no more than a Mediterranean island, he cynically recommended that France might cede Corsica to England; Spain would retain West Florida. The plain fact was that Spain would be as unlikely to part with conquered West Florida as Britain was to part with unconquered Gibraltar.

As long as Spain adhered to her demand for Gibraltar and her determination to continue the war, there was a slight chance that West Florida might revert to British control. Shelburne, Jay, and Vergennes were not averse to British repossession, but Shelburne could not seriously consider West Florida as an equivalent for Gibraltar. If Vergennes wanted peace—and like Choiseul twenty years earlier, he faced a deteriorating military situation and an empty treasury—he must sweeten the pot at the expense of France. He came up with a complicated series of exchanges whereby Spain would retain West Florida and East Florida below Cape Canaveral, but at that point Shelburne admitted that neither his cabinet nor the British public would ever agree to part with Gibraltar, and "to hold up the peace for West Florida would be 'a madness which we can never justify.'"[20] Vergennes begged for terms which he could honorably urge upon the Spanish ambassador, but the decision in London was that Spain must satisfy herself with Minorca, the retention of West Florida, and the acquisition of yet defiant East Florida. Aranda agreed promptly enough to these terms and tried to hide his chagrin over Gibraltar by stressing to Madrid the resultant satisfaction of Spain's colonial and imperial interests. Spain would control the Gulf of Mexico as she had never done before. Her gain was thereby considerable—and considerably more, John Adams growled, than she deserved.

In 1783, as in 1763, peace-making produced some strange diplomatic contortions. Anglo-American hostility concluded in an amity that came near to fulfilling Shelburne's dream of an English-speaking economic union. France, pushed one fateful step closer

20. Morris, *Peacemakers*, p. 401.

to national bankruptcy, finally depended upon Britain to bring her Bourbon ally to the sticking point. Spain could boast that with the Floridas in hand the Gulf of Mexico was virtually a *mare clausum*, but her greatest efforts against Gibraltar had met with humiliating defeat, and modern diplomatic historians would agree that the Spanish acquisition of the Floridas was "a positive advantage to the United States . . . because it replaced the British by a potentially weaker power on that frontier of future expansion."[21] Britain did not bewail her loss. As Shelburne told the House of Lords, East Florida was useless to Britain without West Florida, and none need envy Spain her American neighbor. Seeking to sugar-coat the pill for Charles III, Vergennes had assured Spain that the acquisition of the Gulf coast would secure her American empire for centuries to come, but the last word must rest with Benjamin Vaughan who, having failed to persuade English policy-makers to undertake the recovery of the lost province, gloomily but accurately predicted that Florida was a possession that could not be held long or profitably by any power in the world except the United States.[22]

21. Bemis, *The Diplomacy of the American Revolution,* p. 111.
22. Harlow, *Founding of the Second British Empire,* pp. 360, 436–40.

De Brahm's East Florida on the Eve of Revolution: The Materials for Its Recreation

Louis De Vorsey, Jr.

WILLIAM Gerard De Brahm, British East Florida's first surveyor general, was also the colony's most eminent geographer in the pre–American Revolutionary era. While the primary purpose of this essay is to suggest the historical value of De Brahm's corpus of verbal and cartographic descriptions of East Florida on the eve of the Revolution, a sketch of the man and his colorful career in the colony's most formative period will also be provided.

British East Florida was created as a new colony through the medium of George III's famous omnibus Proclamation of October 7, 1763, which included the following description: "The Government of East Florida bounded to the westward by the Gulph of Mexico and the Apalachicola River; to the northward by a line drawn from that part of the said river where the Chatahouchee and Flint rivers meet, to the source of St. Mary's River, and by the course of the said river to the Atlantick Ocean; and to the eastward and southward by the Atlantick Ocean, and the Gulph of Florida including all islands within six leagues of the sea coast."[1] As Charles L. Mowat has shown, in his study of British East Florida, England's leaders lost no time in their efforts to attract settlers to the new colony.[2] Their efforts and plans suffered, however, since the vast

1. The proclamation was published in full with an illustrative map in the October 1763 issue of *The Gentleman's Magazine* (London). It can also be found in Charles J. Kappler, *Indian Affairs—Laws and Treaties* (Washington, 1903–29), 4:1172, or Merrill Jensen, ed., *American Colonial Documents to 1776*, vol. 9 of *English Historical Documents* (London, 1955), pp. 640–43.
2. "The First Campaign of Publicity for Florida," *Mississippi Valley Historical Review* 30 (December 1943):359–76.

new domain which had been described in the Proclamation of 1763 was at best only vaguely charted and superficially exploited by its original Spanish overlords. To the British, East Florida was *terra incognita* in the fullest sense of that term.

Almost any contemporary British map attempting to show Florida in the 1760s and early 1770s reveals gross errors in even the simple delineation of Florida's general outline. An engraved map by Emanuel Bowen, who had been geographer to George II, can be taken as an example.[3] He had prepared his handsome map in 1763 to illustrate the new territorial divisions of North America. On it, the southern third of the Florida peninsula appears as a fragmented archipelago of large and small islands separated by elongated sounds and large embayments. A symbolic spur of mountains can be traced south from the Appalachians to form a spine of the peninsula. A fanciful St. Johns River is shown breaking the spine and flowing both to the north in its normal course and to the south to empty into the sea by at least two nonexistent southern distributaries.

Perhaps even more widely circulated than the Bowen map was the one which accompanied an "Account of East and West Florida" which appeared in the *Gentleman's Magazine* issue of November 1763 (see Figure 1).[4] The distortions inherent in this map are immediately apparent, with almost all of the Florida peninsula segmented by a skein of waterways and channels. Particularly prominent are the "Bahia del Espiritu Santo" and "Laguna del Espiritu Santo" which are linked to form a continuous broad water body which reaches from present-day Tampa to the Atlantic Ocean at "Boca de Ratones." A similar channel is also shown on the Bowen map. This is a feature which had emerged on the maps of the first decade of the eighteenth century and only disappeared after half a century.[5]

Such was the character of practically all British cartography attempting to show East Florida immediately following its accretion to the North American empire of George III. Nor were things

3. Emanuel Bowen, "An Accurate Map of North America Describing and Distinguishing the British, Spanish, and French Dominions on This Great Continent According to the Definitive Treaty Concluded at Paris 10th February 1763."

4. For a discussion of this map, see William P. Cumming, *The Southeast in Early Maps* (Chapel Hill, 1962), p. 233.

5. See plates 45, 47, and 56, ibid., for examples.

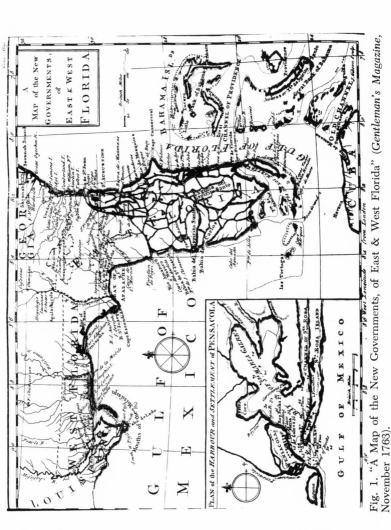

Fig. 1. "A Map of the New Governments, of East & West Florida" (*Gentleman's Magazine*, November 1763).

greatly improved when Dr. William Stork produced his engraved map in about 1767.[6] One contemporary bitterly complained of that "wretched Map of Doctr. Stork, which is not only Imaginary, but might as well serve for any part of Germany as for East Florida."[7] At least the archipelago effect is removed from southern Florida in the Stork rendition. A large lake is included, doubtlessly Lake Okeechobee. Bernard Romans later observed, "this lake has given rise to the intersected and mangled condition in which we see the peninsula exhibited in old maps."[8] Romans' own famous map of 1775 shows an unequivocably peninsular Florida.[9]

Royal advisors and administrators, both in London and America, felt a pressing need for accurate maps and detailed geographic information as they began to grapple with the enormous task of organizing and developing Britain's vast new territorial acquisitions in America. In a communication to the King,[10] early in 1764, the British Board of Trade admitted, "We find ourselves under the greatest difficulties arising from the want of exact surveys of these countries in America many parts of which have never been surveyed at all, and others so imperfectly that the charts and maps thereof are not to be depended upon." The King's chief advisory panel further observed that "In this situation, we are reduced to the necessity of making representation to your majesty founded upon little or no information or of delaying the important service of settling these parts of your majesty's dominions." Such a state of affairs was clearly intolerable. The board concluded its communication with a recommendation: "In the strongest manner that no time should be lost in obtaining accurate surveys of all your majesty's North American dominions, but more especially of such parts as from their natural advantages require our immediate attention." Predictably, these parts last mentioned were designated as Atlantic Canada and the peninsula of East Florida.

To implement these much needed accurate surveys, two new ad-

6. William Stork, "A New Map of Florida," ca. 1767.
7. Charles Bernard, quoted by Charles L. Mowat in "The First Campaign of Publicity for Florida," p. 375.
8. *A Concise Natural History of East and West Florida* (Gainesville, 1962), p. 286.
9. For a discussion of Romans' large engraved map of Florida, see P. Lee Phillips, *Notes on the Life and Works of Bernard Romans* (DeLand, Fla., 1924), pp. 18–23.
10. British Public Record Office, Exchequer and Audit Department Records, Accounts, Various, vol. 140, no page; hereafter A.O. 3–140, no page.

ministrative units were created in America: the Northern and Southern Survey Districts divided by the Potomac River. A surveyor general was appointed for each district and charged with the responsibility of conducting detailed geographical surveys. Captain Samuel Holland, the accomplished military engineer and cartographer then active in the St. Lawrence Valley, became the surveyor general for the northern district.[11] To fill the southern surveyorship the Board of Trade chose William Gerard De Brahm, then serving as one of the two provincial surveyors of lands for the colony of Georgia. He was also an engineer-cartographer with a military background and considerable local experience.[12] In July 1764, De Brahm's commission as a joint surveyor general of Georgia was terminated, when he received this new appointment as surveyor general of East Florida and surveyor general of the southern district.

Although many authorities have identified De Brahm as a native of Holland, the records show that he was born in Germany in 1718 and was left fatherless at the age of six.[13] Just where and how he was educated is not revealed by any of the materials available in British or American archives. It is hoped that future research in Germany will provide information on this phase in the life of one of eighteenth-century Florida's most colorful historical figures. That he received an excellent education in classical and modern languages, mathematics, history, literature, biblical studies, and the

11. For a discussion of Holland's life and career, see Willis Chipman, "The Life and Times of Major Samuel Holland, Surveyor General, 1764–1801," *Ontario Historical Society Papers and Records* 21 (1924):11–90.

12. For details on De Brahm's career, see Louis De Vorsey, Jr., *De Brahm's Report of the General Survey in the Southern District of North America* (Columbia, S.C., 1971).

13. Notable among these are Carita Doggett Corse and Charles L. Mowat. See Corse's "De Brahm's Report on East Florida, 1773," and Mowat's "That Odd Being De Brahm" in vols. 17 and 20 respectively of the *Florida Historical Quarterly*. The exact date and place of De Brahm's birth are revealed on a small gold medal which bears his family coat of arms; it is now owned by the St. Augustine Historical Society. I am grateful to Mr. J. Carver of St. Augustine for bringing this unusual source of information to my attention. The medal is inscribed "These are the Arms of JOHN WILLIAM GERARD de BRAHM Knight Legium to the Roman Empire; Born August the 20th 1718, at COBLENCE in the Electorate of TRIER; formerly Captain Engineer to CHARLES VII. Roman Emperor; now Surveyor General for the Southern District of North America to His Majesty GEORGE III. King of Great Britain; who Presents this as a Memorial to his Dearest Grand Daughter Frances Mulcaster, the First of January MDCCLXXVIII."

burgeoning experimental sciences of the day is amply proved by his later performances in America.

Professor Mowat recognized De Brahm's attainments and described him as "a man whose versatility of genius went beyond even that of the typical 18th century dilettante, a surveyor, engineer, botanist, astronomer, meteorologist, student of ocean currents, alchemist, sociologist, historian and mystical philosopher."[14] De Brahm described his father as "an admirer of natural philosophy" and a devotee of alchemy, a pursuit common in the eighteenth century.[15] The younger De Brahm continued to maintain an active interest in alchemical research throughout his own long life. It is not surprising, in view of the unsettled political conditions which characterized central Europe during the first half of the eighteenth century, to discover that De Brahm found an outlet for his talents in an army career in the service of Emperor Charles VII. He saw action in eleven campaigns, in Germany, Turkey, and France, under Prince Eugene, Count Wallis, and Count Seckendorf.

In 1748, the thirty-year-old De Brahm resigned his commission as a captain-engineer in the Emperor's army. At about the same time, he renounced the Roman Catholic faith and was, in his own words, "persecuted, and banished" from the Bavarian Palatinate as a result.[16] Like many other South German Protestants, De Brahm was befriended by the Bishop of Augsburg, Samuel Urlsperger. The bishop was one of two foreign members on the predominantly English Board of Trustees for Establishing the Colony of Georgia in America, and was actively promoting the colony by encouraging displaced Germans to settle there. Through his good offices in the summer of 1751, De Brahm the exile found himself in charge of a group of 156 German Protestants on their way to settle at Ebenezer in Georgia. The Reverend Urlsperger was sufficiently impressed by De Brahm to pay his passage to Ebenezer, "in hopes that he will give service to the colony in general and to the settlement in particular."[17] On both of these scores the bishop was more than amply rewarded.

14. "That Odd Being De Brahm," p. 323.
15. Staffordshire County Record Office, Stafford, England, Dartmouth Manuscripts D177811 617; hereafter Dartmouth Ms. D177811 617.
16. British Public Record Office, Exchequer and Audit Department Records, Claims, American Loyalists, Series II; hereafter A.O. 13–137, p. 126.
17. British Public Record Office, Colonial Office Records, America and West Indies, vol. 372, p. 281; hereafter C.O. 5–372, p. 281.

De Brahm's skill as a surveyor and cartographer was quickly appreciated by his contemporaries engaged in the settlement of the Georgia wilderness. In more recent years, workers in historical cartography have come to share this appreciation of his talents. William P. Cumming, author of *The Southeast in Early Maps*, describes De Brahm's first printed map as "far superior to any cartographical work for the Southern District that had gone before" (p. 54), and he further observes that "with De Brahm, we turn from the amateur to the professional, from the general outlines of the region to topographical accuracy." De Brahm was not content merely to survey a plot of land and to draw a rough sketch or plat of the survey, the common practice of most land surveyors then as now. Rather, he showed the essential quality of a geographer in his approach to surveying. He was more interested in the larger whole of the landscape of which the individual landholdings surveyed were only fragments. De Brahm's mind was always searching for broad patterns in nature, and once these patterns were perceived, he speculated as to their possible causes and effects. While he traveled and conducted these early land measurements, he was observing and recording regional differences in such things as landform patterns, climate, soils, flora, fauna, and land use in the Southeast.

De Brahm's reputation soon carried beyond Georgia to attract the attention of James Glen, South Carolina's royal governor. Glen invited him to design a system of fortifications to insure the security of Charleston. The death of South Carolina's surveyor general during the summer of 1755 created a vacancy, and Glen issued De Brahm an interim appointment to the post. In 1756, when the opportunity arose to construct a fort in the heart of Cherokee tribal lands, De Brahm was selected to design and supervise its construction. This was the ill-fated Fort Loudoun, transmontane outpost of colonial South Carolina in what is now Monroe County, Tennessee.

In 1754, De Brahm and Henry Yonge were appointed joint surveyors general of lands for the royal colony of Georgia. Georgia's governor—like his counterpart in neighboring South Carolina—recognized De Brahm's standing as a military engineer and strategist and called upon him to assist in drawing up a comprehensive system of fortifications for the defense of the colony. The record shows that William Gerard De Brahm quickly attained a position of considerable influence and responsibility in the colony of Georgia as he had in South Carolina. He served the colony as a military engineer, justice of the peace, cartographer, tax collector, and commissioner for the repair and construction of fortifications. De Brahm seems to have owned considerable property and to have been recognized as a gentleman of standing and responsibility in both Georgia and South Carolina prior to his arrival in the new colony of East Florida.

De Brahm's ability and talents were further recognized in 1764 when he was appointed surveyor general of lands for East Florida and surveyor general for the southern district. In the latter office, he was to be in charge of geographical survey and mapping efforts in "all his majesty's territories on the continent of North America which lie to the south of the Potomac River." Within this vast area first priority was placed upon the mapping of the Florida peninsula. De Brahm was admonished to be accurate and comprehensive in his work since he would be providing, in the words of the official correspondence, "in great measure the guide, by which His Majesty and his servants are to form their judgements upon the different proposals that shall be offered for making settlements upon these coasts."[18]

In the early weeks of 1765, De Brahm moved to St. Augustine where he began his comprehensive geographical reconnaissance of Florida. For the next six years, aided by a number of assistants and deputies, he devoted himself to this task. He conducted numerous surveying expeditions by sea and on land—on the St. Johns River, which carried him south to the Florida Keys, and along the Gulf coast to Tampa Bay. From his St. Augustine base, he also explored and mapped the country to the north as far as the St. Marys River which formed the boundary with Georgia. His penetrations of the interior were frequently limited by fears of Indian attack, but he managed to survey high up the St. Marys toward its source in Okeefenokee Swamp, almost all of eastern Florida between the St. Johns River and the Atlantic Ocean, and the coastal fringe and islands around to Tampa Bay. Hurricanes, shipwrecks, attacks of fever, Indian threats, and official opposition all made De Brahm's labors more arduous. His surveys were very meticulous and scientific. Frequent astronomic observations were taken on land to fix

18. C.O. 324–17, dated August 15, 1764.

positions and to determine the degree and direction of compass error in the areas surveyed. Astronomic fixes were also used to determine linear distances which were compared with distances determined with the surveyor's chain over land traverses. In inaccessible locations, such as the Florida Keys, local baselines were determined with the chain and trigonometric techniques which were used to complete the survey. (Figure 2 shows the areas of present-day Florida explored and mapped by De Brahm.)

Many detailed maps and charts were prepared by De Brahm and his deputies from 1765 to 1771. These, along with his letters and his official report to George III, form an important source of information on Florida at a time when the available records of Indian and Spanish colonial occupation were relatively sparse. De Brahm's general survey of East Florida was terminated in 1771 when he was ordered to London to answer charges of malfeasance lodged by East Florida Governor James Grant.[19] De Brahm was eventually exonerated, but his plan to continue the survey of East Florida was blocked by the outbreak of the American Revolution. Even his naval sloop, *Cherokee,* was commandeered for military duties upon his return to Charleston in the autumn of 1775.

Although he was unable to complete the full project, the results of De Brahm's completed surveys were far-reaching in their influence. They met with the approbation of George III and his principal North American advisors, as well as leaders of the eighteenth-century scientific communities in Europe and America. Aspects of De Brahm's work reached broad audiences through such published volumes as his Florida sailing directions, *The Atlantic Pilot.* This intriguing book appeared in English in 1772 and in French in 1788, and is one of the volumes in the Bicentennial Floridiana Facsimile Series published by the University Presses of Florida for the Florida Bicentennial Commission. Although Bernard Romans had scathingly criticized De Brahm's work in his own book, he joined De Brahm's findings with those of other navigators in his 1797 volume entitled *A New and Enlarged Book of Sailing Directions.*[20] This

19. For accounts of the Grant–De Brahm feud see Mowat, "That Odd Being De Brahm," and De Vorsey, *De Brahm's Report,* esp. pp. 40–43.

20. *Natural History of East and West Florida,* pp. 267, 273, 286, 288, 292, 295, and 296–300; *A New and Enlarged Book of Sailing Directions . . . Gulf and Windward Pilot . . . Also the Additions of Captains W. G. Debrahm, Bishop, Hester, Archibald Dalzel, Esq., George Gauld, Esq., Lieut. Woodriffe and Other Experienced Navigators* (London, 1797).

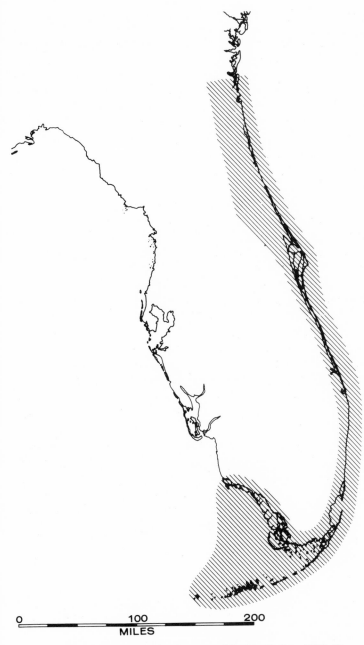

0   100   200
MILES

Fig. 2. Extent of Florida mapped by De Brahm, 1765–71.

was indeed a tribute since Romans, De Brahm's sometime deputy, was one of the surveyor general's severest critics. During the American Revolution, many followed the military events with the aid of "A General Map of the Southern British Colonies in America" which had a wide circulation. His map was included in the *American Military Pocket Atlas,* prepared for His Majesty's naval and army officers serving in the American theater.[21] It acknowledged De Brahm's contributions. His hydrographic surveys along the southern coasts were employed by Joseph Frederick Walet De Barres, the creator of the revolutionary era's cartographic *opus magnum,* the well-known *Atlantic Neptune.*[22]

In the early decades of the nineteenth century, many experts commented favorably on De Brahm's surveys of Florida. Among these were the famous surveyor of the Florida-Georgia boundary Andrew Ellicott,[23] and the author James Grant Forbes, whose volume *Sketches, Historical and Topographical of the Floridas* was published in 1821 and reprinted in the Floridiana Facsimile and Reprint Series, University of Florida Press, in 1964.[24] There is also evidence that an original manuscript copy of De Brahm's report and maps provided valuable information to United States government figures concerned with the development of Florida during the middle years of the nineteenth century.[25] Certainly Buckingham Smith was familiar with certain of De Brahm's works and made frequent allusions to them in his own writings.[26] It is also very

21. *The American Military Pocket Atlas; Being An Approved Collection of Correct Maps, Both General and Particular, of the British Colonies, Especially Those Which Now Are, Or Probably May Be The Theatre of War; Taken Principally From The Actual Surveys and Judicious Observations of Engineers De Brahm and Romans; Cook, Jackson and Collet; Maj. Holland and Other Officers, Employed In His Majesty's Fleets and Armies* (London, [1776]).

22. For a review of Des Barres' full and colorful life, see G.N.D. Evans, *Uncommon Obdurate: The Several Public Careers of J.F.W. Des Barres* (Toronto, 1969).

23. Andrew Ellicott, *The Journal of Andrew Ellicott* (Philadelphia, 1803, reprint), p. 257.

24. *Sketches, Historical and Topographical of the Floridas; More Particularly of East Florida* (New York, 1821), p. 97.

25. See, for example, the March 10 and 12, 1848, memoranda by James D. Westcott which accompany the Harvard University copy of De Brahm's original manuscript, "Report of the General Survey in the Southern District of North America," now in the Houghton Library Collection.

26. "Report of Buckingham Smith, Esq. June 1, 1848," *Senate Documents,* 30th Cong., 1st sess., Rep. Comm. no. 242, August 12, 1848, quoted in Phillips, *Notes on the Life and Works of Bernard Romans,* pp. 15–17.

possible that De Brahm's materials influenced American policy formulation on Florida after its accession from Spain in 1821.

During the twentieth century, De Brahm's work fell into relative obscurity. This fact was noted by H. Roy Merrens in his paper "The Physical Environment of Early America,"[27] and he suggested that the relative inaccessibility of De Brahm's material has resulted in his obscurity. This condition has been somewhat rectified recently, and the corpus of De Brahm's original materials are available now to the scholar devoted to the study of Florida on the eve of the American Revolution.

The extant De Brahm materials relevant to the study of eighteenth-century East Florida are found in four categories in several British and American archives: (1) the first-hand reports which De Brahm forwarded from Florida to his superiors in London; (2) the large-scale 1769 compiled map of East Florida; (3) De Brahm's "Report of the General Survey in the Southern District of North America" and the associated large maps of East Florida; and (4) the De Brahm material in the Earl of Dartmouth's papers. Each of these categories will be discussed in an attempt to suggest their potential value to scholars concerned with British East Florida in this period.

(1) These original materials are collected in two major archives, the Library of Congress and the British Public Record Office. The Library of Congress materials are sometimes ignored by historians since they are primarily cartographic in character and are housed in the library's Geography and Map Division in Alexandria, Virginia.[28]

Figure 3 is one of De Brahm's earliest maps of East Florida, received in London during the summer of 1765. It is a valuable source of data concerning the natural conditions of the area at that time. Vegetative types and conditions are indicated by symbolic and verbal means. Depth soundings and bottom conditions as well as water color are clearly shown. The Gulf Stream and its inshore countercurrent are clearly depicted, perhaps for the first time on a British map of this scale. A detailed verbal description of the area and the phenomena mapped is included on the left-hand side. There is an

27. "The Physical Environment of Early America: Images and Image Makers in Colonial South Carolina," *The Geographical Review* 59 (October 1969):530–56.
28. P. L. Phillips, *The Lowery Collection* (Washington, 1912), pp. 340–41.

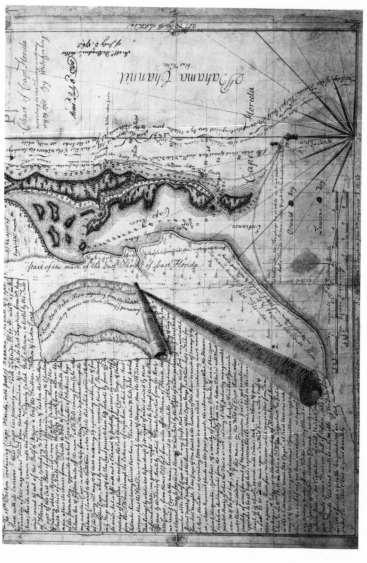

Fig. 3. "Chart of Cape Florida according to the Surveys made May 13 & 29 1765. By W. G. de Brahm."

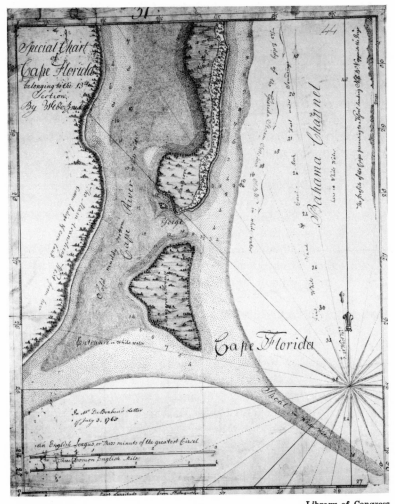

Fig. 4. "Special Chart of Cape Florida belonging to the 13th Section. By W. G. de Brahm."

artistic scrolling effect De Brahm accomplished with his drawing pen.

Figure 4 is a larger scale depiction of the same area, centering on the navigation channel into Biscayne Bay. It is clearly a navigation chart and is less valuable in terms of terrestrial detail. There is a profile view of the entrance to Biscayne Bay which appears along the upper right-hand margin of the chart. Like the preceding map, longitudes on this chart are expressed in terms of degrees and minutes east of the St. Augustine meridian.

These two maps are not to be found in the British Public Record Office. Apparently De Brahm's superiors in London were a bit overwhelmed by the material which he transmitted from his Florida surveys, and they forwarded his maps and charts from this early period to the Board of Admirality. Sometime during the nineteenth century, Peter Force acquired these materials, and eventually they became part of the Library of Congress collection. This is the first time that either of these maps has been reproduced.

The British Public Record Office has the bulk of De Brahm's official letters, reports, and memorials. Unfortunately some of the originals are in a poor state of repair and are breaking. A detailed description of these verbal materials would require more space than is available here, so only one will be described. This is a twenty-page letter which De Brahm addressed to the Board of Trade on April 4, 1765.[29] It is, in effect, the report of his first explorations in East Florida. This lengthy document presents a detailed account which begins with a sketch of St. Augustine and its environs, proceeds to an account of the progress of the coastal survey to the south, the entry into Muskito (present-day Ponce de Leon) Inlet and its exploration before the establishment of New Smyrna, and ends with an exciting account of a hurricane-like storm which threatened the surveyors' lives. It is a document rich in its content and fascinating in its construction. He comments on the Gulf Stream off this coast. The region which was soon to become New Smyrna and one of East Florida's chief population centers is described, with references to the soils, flora, and fauna as well as the impressive shell mounds left by aboriginal dwellers.

(2) In 1769, John and Samuel Lewis, draftsmen to the Plantation Office in London, compiled a map of East Florida from De Brahm's forwarded sketches and surveys. It measures eighteen feet

29. C.O. 323–18, pp. 168–78.

in length, and is now deposited in the British Museum's Map Room. It is an elegant production, and it was in all probability especially prepared for George III's own use. It is catalogued as a part of the King's Topographic Collection (CXXII, 81).[30]

The title of this map is "A Plan of Part of the Coast of East Florida Including St. John's River from an Actual Survey by William Gerard De Brahm, Esquire, Surveyor General of the Southern District of North America." It is drawn to a scale of approximately one inch to one and one-quarter miles, and it is rich in historical detail. In addition to many natural features it shows the location and extent of the land holdings of most of East Florida's original British grantees. The whole of East Florida from the Atlantic shore to the St. Johns River is shown from Amelia Island south to present-day St. Lucie Inlet.

(3) Also housed in the British Museum (Manuscripts Division) is the detailed comprehensive report on his surveys and experiences in the southern colonies which De Brahm personally presented to George III in 1772. This manuscript, catalogued as Kings Ms. 210 & 211, has been edited and was published by the University of South Carolina Press in its South Carolina Tricentennial series under the title *De Brahm's Report of the General Survey in the Southern District of North America*. It is of value to Florida scholars since most of the material is devoted to the colony of East Florida. Fifteen of its twenty-nine original maps and sketches show areas and features in East Florida. The map of "Mukoso Inlet & Environs," presented here as Figure 5 and showing the area of present-day Ponce de Leon Inlet and New Smyrna Beach, is one of these. It is of interest since it shows the "Place intended For the Town of Smyrnea" which became the settlement for Dr. Andrew Turnbull's colony of 1,500 Mediterraneans in 1768.[31] Of particular interest to many with genealogical interests will be De Brahm's "A List of the Inhabitants of East Florida, their Employs, Business and Qualifications in Science from 1763 to 1771," also included in the East Florida section of his report.

30. *Catalogue of the Manuscript Maps, Charts, and Plans, and of the Topographical Drawings in the British Museum* (London, 1891), 3:511.

31. For information on this settlement sixty miles south of St. Augustine, see Carita D. Corse, *Dr. Andrew Turnbull and the New Smyrna Colony of Florida* (Jacksonville, 1919); E. P. Panagopoulos, *New Smyrna: An Eighteenth Century Greek Odyssey* (Gainesville, 1966); Bruno Roselli, *The Italians in Colonial Florida* (Jacksonville, 1940).

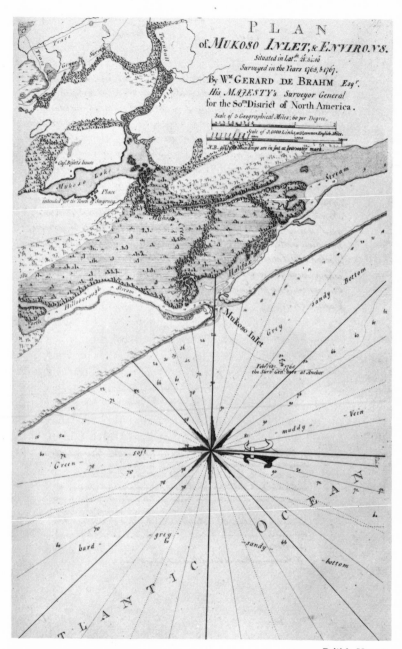

Fig. 5. "Plan of Mukoso Inlet & Environs . . . Surveyed in the Years 1765, & 1767. By Gerard de Brahm Esq[r]. His MAJESTY's Surveyor General for the So[rn]. District of North America."

During the time that De Brahm was in London composing his report to the King, he was also busily preparing his own large-scale maps of East Florida. Housed in the British Public Record Office, they are very large and detailed. Northern East Florida is portrayed on the map titled "A Survey of the Part of the Eastern Coast of East Florida from St. Mary's Inlet to Mount Halifax. Showing the Ascertained Boundary Between East Florida and the Creek Indians." This map is almost four and one-half feet wide by about six feet in length and is catalogued as Colonial Office Map 700/Florida 53, in the Public Record Office.

Southern East Florida, all the way to the Keys, is shown on an even larger map titled "East Florida East of the 82nd Degree of Longitude from the Meridian of London Pursuant to the Directions from the Right Honorable The Lords of Trade and Plantations. Surveyed By William Gerard de Brahm Surveyor General for the Southern District of North America." This map is approximately five feet wide and twenty feet long and is catalogued as Colonial Office Map 700/Florida 3 in the same archive.

In addition to the British Museum copy of De Brahm's comprehensive "Report," there is another in the Houghton Library at Harvard University. This copy was De Brahm's personal set which he retained until 1798, the year before his death. De Brahm delivered these materials to Phineas Bond, the British Consul in Philadelphia. In time they were acquired in England by Henry Stevens, who sold them to Harvard in 1848. This manuscript is very similar, although not identical, to the British Museum version. Virtually all of the De Brahm material discussed by Florida scholars Carita Doggett Corse and Charles L. Mowat was derived from this important source.[32]

(4) De Brahm began a correspondence with the Earl of Dartmouth as early as 1769. During the period in which De Brahm was in London preparing his defense against Governor Grant's charges of malfeasance, Dartmouth replaced Hillsborough as secretary of state for the Southern Department and became De Brahm's patron and protector. Dartmouth had a deep interest in American affairs, particularly in Florida land speculation and colonization schemes. Included in these schemes was one to locate a large group of Swiss and other Protestants on Dartmouth's huge land grant in southern Florida, in the vicinity of present-day Miami. De Brahm personally

32. See note 13.

devoted energy and time to efforts to persuade the group to enter an agreement to settle on Dartmouth's grant.

As a result of the close relationship existing between Dartmouth and De Brahm, centering as it did on Florida lands, scholars concerned with the colony and its people on the eve of the American Revolution can ill afford to overlook the Dartmouth–De Brahm materials.[33] They are available for study at the Staffordshire County Record Office, Stafford, England, and copies are in the P. K. Yonge Library of Florida History, University of Florida. Of interest in this collection is De Brahm's detailed description of the Miami region with his recommendations on how to succeed in settling in the area. This item is entitled "To the Cape Florida Society."[34] Many other sources related to Florida are in the Dartmouth Manuscripts and they invite the attention of Floridians with an interest in the state's rich history.

These four categories form the bulk of the corpus of largely first-hand historical and geographical evidence which British East Florida's first surveyor general compiled during his six years in the colony.[35] It seems appropriate to conclude this brief essay with the concluding sentence of Professor Mowat's article "That Odd Being De Brahm." He wrote, "Certainly the small community of East Florida, which contained a greater number of original minds than its size or infancy entitled it to, had no figure more noteworthy than that of its Surveyor General." It seems appropriate also to suggest here that De Brahm bequeathed present-day Floridians a rich legacy of little-used historical and geographical source materials— source materials from which the scholar or interested reader may re-create a surprisingly complete and detailed image of British East Florida as it was on the eve of the American Revolution. Such a re-creation seems essential if we of the present are to realistically attempt to understand that climactic period and its people.

33. Historical Manuscripts Commission, *The Manuscripts of the Earl of Dartmouth, American Papers,* 3 vols. (London, 1887–96).

34. Dartmouth Ms. D177811 607.

35. The Lilly Library of Indiana University holds a lengthy De Brahm manuscript entitled "1773 Report of the General Survey in the Southern District of North America: To the Right Honorable Earl of Dartmouth, His Majesty's Principal Secretary of State for the American Department." This contains a large amount of material on Florida which appears to be very similar to portions of the unpublished "Report" cited in note 12.

Commentary

PAUL H. SMITH

RECENTLY I have talked with several persons who have expressed surprise that Florida was planning to hold Bicentennial Symposia. Their surprise illustrates, I believe, both why Florida must be involved in such Bicentennial observances, and the limitations of many Americans' conception of the American Revolutionary era. It is clear, at any rate, that scholars interested in the approaching Bicentennial face both an opportunity and a great challenge. The opportunity is frankly one of education, of disseminating information about this area of North America during that brief, formative, revolutionary era. The challenge, however, is not so simple, for it involves not the mere accumulation of more information, but conceptualization, interpretation, understanding.

These two papers are primarily directed to the former enterprise: they add more to our specific knowledge of the Floridas during the period of the American Revolution than to our general understanding of the place of Florida in the developments of the last third of the eighteenth century. They are not primarily directed at using a specific subject to illuminate a larger event—which to me, as a historian preoccupied with the Bicentennial, is the break-up of a great empire and the birth of a new nation. To be fair to Professors Rea and De Vorsey, they were not asked or expected to undertake that larger task. They were not given time to attempt it. But while I do not believe that task was their responsibility, I do believe that it is your responsibility. Rather, it is our responsibility— the responsibility of all who have participated in this symposium and those who will read in published form the papers that have been presented. In short, it ought to be the purpose of Bicentennial activities to stimulate a general rethinking of the Revolution, and it is a preoccupation with this larger aim I find to be generally underemphasized today.

Focusing first on Professor Rea's paper, I believe it would be well to remind ourselves that West Florida, as it has been considered here, did not exist 300 years ago or 100 years ago, but of course it did exist 200 years ago. This in turn suggests the limitation of attempting to study West Florida as an entity, separated from the "times": West Florida existed only in the context of its times.

Thus we are reminded that West Florida was created at a given moment, obviously in response to some needs, and those needs quite clearly had considerable bearing on the diplomacy of the period. It is the comparative neglect of consideration of those needs that I find puzzling. To gauge how West Florida would be discussed at the peace tables, one should know more precisely what specific value various nations attached to it, and what concrete steps were taken from time to time to ensure its future possession. Furthermore, we must know not only why West Florida was desired, but also what alternatives were perceived when it was being evaluated. Such an inquiry would lead us to the relative value of West Florida in comparison to retention of the Falkland Islands, of Minorca, Gibraltar, Cuba, or of rights to the North Atlantic fisheries, cutting logwood in Honduras, and free navigation of the Mississippi. And surely such an inquiry would lead us to recognize that these many variables changed from time to time with conditions and events.

My evaluation of Professor Rea's paper hinges, therefore, somewhat unfairly on what he did not do today, rather than on what he did. Failure to give sufficient attention to various alternatives to possession of West Florida—such as I have catalogued, and which I am sure contemporary diplomats did consider carefully—plus slighting the reasons why Britain considered Florida a valuable prize, yet did not retain it after 1783, suggest opportunities for filling in the story and improving our overall understanding of the period. To broaden the discussion in these directions, which I am sure Professor Rea considered, and then deliberately—but mistakenly, I believe—slighted, would require further evaluation of a variety of strategic and economic factors. These in turn require study of matters as disparate as eighteenth-century transportation routes, demography, and various imperial administrative problems. And beyond immediate military and economic considerations we encounter the related subjects of managing the great southern Indian tribes, supplying and managing the Illinois country, and guiding the ever pressing stream of land-hungry settlers. For these factors, I must refer the interested student to the recent works of J. Leitch Wright (*Anglo-Spanish Rivalry in North America*), Robert L. Gold (*Borderland Empires in Transition: The Triple-Nation Transfer of Florida*), and even to Cecil Johnson's older study of West Florida. To these I must add the paper Professor Rea prepared for publication for this symposium, because what was presented is approximately half the longer paper I was privileged to read, a much abler and understandably more comprehensive work. What the author presented at the symposium he termed an "exploratory essay"; I would label it a "tantalizing summary." It is the full essay which is included in this published work, and in his Introduction to the facsimile edition of Phillip Pittman's *The Present State of the European Settlements on the Missisippi*, published in 1974 in the Bicentennial Floridiana Facsimile Series, by the University Presses of Florida.

On Professor De Vorsey's subject, we have the advantage of confronting a more compact topic, and one not so full of the pitfalls of definition and delimitation. His recent publications on De Brahm—which I recommend highly—have certainly rescued De Brahm from relative obscurity, and have placed geographers and historians alike in his debt. His research into De Brahm's early career is impressive, and the energy shown in tracking down De Brahm's cartographic work deserves unqualified praise. Indeed, Professor De Vorsey has been too modest in assessing his role in calling attention to the various portions of the corpus of De Brahm's work, particularly that found in the Geography and Map Division at the Library of Congress.

Let me note here that Professor De Vorsey accomplished that task about a year before the Library of Congress undertook the reconstituting of the magnificent Peter Force Collection, which was acquired in 1867 but was subsequently distributed through the various library divisions, obscuring the original identity of the papers. Only recently, after Professor De Vorsey did his research, has the library rediscovered, from Force's personal papers, what was in the original collection. While it is difficult to consult much of De Brahm's original cartographic work in the United Kingdom, his extensive correspondence is more readily available, and this is the portion that historians will most likely want to consult. The Library of Congress has almost all of the pertinent Public Record Office materials on microfilm, available to most researchers on interlibrary loan, and the P. K. Yonge Library of Florida History at the University of Florida has nearly all the pertinent East and West Florida Public Record Office volumes for those who have access to its resources. Finally, the Geography and Map Division of the Library of Congress is quite accessible, and it has a larger staff, better working quarters, and more available parking facilities than the main building of the Library of Congress.

The rest of my comments simply confirm that the interests of historians and geographers are often significantly different. I want to call attention to a few examples of how study of De Brahm's life and career in America might improve our general understanding of the Anglo-American empire in the Revolutionary era. De Brahm's early career, for example, certainly illustrates the cultural diversity of the southern colonies in the eighteenth century, and shows that talented men of diverse backgrounds could rise to remarkably important official positions of influence in the imperial system. Since De Brahm's experience was typical of what prevailed through the technical services—both military and nonmilitary—it suggests an open quality pervading the empire that is often overlooked when one concentrates too exclusively upon the restrictive policies that came to dominate the Anglo-American debate in the 1770s. (One might also note the Quebec Act and contemporaneous policy in India in this connection.) Moreover, notwithstanding De Vorsey's clarification of De Brahm's charting activities, his influence as the provincial surveyor on the settlement of Florida, and consequently on economic, social, and political groupings, needs to be more fully explored. Also the fact that De Brahm held joint appointments—as surveyor general of the southern district of North America and as provincial surveyor general—shows the problem of plural office-holding. That in turn also suggests the parsimonious character of British colonial policy in the 1760s; De Brahm's cartographic work was underfunded, and he felt he had to compensate himself from the fees collected as perquisites of his office as provincial surveyor. Not unexpectedly, controversy over that issue seriously hampered the surveying of East Florida, delayed its settlement, and stimulated factionalism in the province. His anomalous position also illustrates the fragmentation of authority that often characterized the empire and undermined efforts to wield authority efficiently and fairly in the provinces: he held his one commission directly from the Crown, and was answerable only to authority in London for that post, but as provincial surveyor he had also to answer to the governor and the council. This, of course, contributed to his dispute with Governor Grant and his suspension and recall to London to answer charges in person. That episode was the subject of a study by Charles L. Mowat in 1941, and De Vorsey wisely chose to pass over it lightly, but he has also distorted the issue when he writes cryptically of "the eventually exonerated De Brahm." That exoneration was a very ambiguous matter. In this connection historians would like to know just what role Lord Dartmouth played in De Brahm's eventual reinstatement—which occurred four years after his dismissal, and on the eve of Dartmouth's resignation as American secretary—and historians need to know as well what influence De Brahm's previous activities in behalf of Dartmouth's land claims in Florida had on his controversy with Grant and the governor's supporters in the council. I am not saying that Professor De Vorsey is unaware of these issues, but only that he slighted them, and that, if one judges simply from this paper, he is unlikely to sense the rich opportunities available in further study of De Brahm.

On the other hand, De Vorsey particularly deserves commendation for focusing on the rich De Brahm material in the Dartmouth papers. There is much De Brahm material that awaits study, especially his correspondence, other than his cartographic work. In B. F. Stevens' 180-volume manuscript index to materials in British depositories, which was copied for the Library of Congress just for the years 1763 to 1783, there are seven pages of entries under De Brahm's name. In view of the extraordinary diversity of De Brahm's life and the extent of the materials available bearing on certain significant portions of his activities, it will be unfortunate indeed if interest in his cartographic work should deter scholars from pursuing topics related to other aspects of this remarkable man's career.

Architecture in Eighteenth-Century West Florida

SAMUEL WILSON, JR.

LITTLE has survived from the eighteenth century to the present day of the numerous houses, forts, and public buildings erected by the French and Spanish in their colonial frontier areas of East and West Florida. In all the vast extent of this territory, from the Atlantic coast to the Mississippi River, to the northern border of Florida and the northern border of eastern Louisiana (excluding the Isle of Orleans and the city of New Orleans), very few structures remain that can be positively documented as dating from this century that encompassed almost the beginning and almost the end of European settlement in the Gulf coastal region. Thus, to understand and appreciate the architecture of this colonial period, it is necessary to rely largely on drawings and documents in French and Spanish archives and on some surviving structures of the period that are beyond but near the area in question.

The French began settlement in 1699, when Pierre LeMoyne d'Iberville established Fort Maurepas on Biloxi Bay, the year after Andres de Arriola founded a new colony at Pensacola.[1] Iberville's fort is well documented in his journals[2] and, according to the plan attributed to his engineer, Remy Reno,[3] he employed many of the

1. William Bridgewater and Elizabeth J. Sherwood, eds., *The Columbia Encyclopedia*, 2d ed. (New York, 1950), p. 1513.
2. Pierre Margry, *Decouvertes et etablissements des francais dans le sud de l'Amerique septentionale (1614–1754)* (Paris, 1879–82), 4:125, 195–98, 447.
3. Paris, Service Hydrographique de la Marine, Atlas 4044–C. f. 68. Illustrated in Samuel Wilson, Jr., *Bienville's New Orleans* (New Orleans, n.d. [1968]), p. 6.

construction techniques that were to be used in the area throughout the French colonial period. Two of the fort's four bastions were of *pièce sur pièce*, heavy squared timbers laid horizontally, one upon another, dovetailed at the corners to form a rigid and solid wall. The other two bastions were of *poteaux en terre*, "good palisades, well doubled . . . made of such heavy stakes that it takes four men to carry them. . . ."

These construction methods were employed in the first buildings erected at Fort Louis when the French transferred their center of activity to the banks of the Mobile River in 1702. The largest of these structures was described in a 1704 report as "a house 68 feet long by 16 wide, with an upper story, of *piece sur piece*, of squared wood, with a roof of timber framing, roofed with shingles, and a gallery from end to end. . . ."[4] Other buildings were described as being of *charpente* (timber framing) and a small warehouse was of *pieux debout* (upright stakes). A brick kiln was also established at Fort Louis, probably for supplying bricks for chimneys; this material did not come into common use for building until nearly 1730. Stone was practically unknown as a building material in the French colony, although orders were issued from Versailles to a Captain Bajot in 1715 for the construction of a fort at Dauphin Island which "His Majesty wishes . . . might be constructed of masonry. . . . The stone for the construction of the masonry shall be taken from the nearest spot which is said to be on the other side of the bay towards the Spanish fort of Pensacola."[5] Actually nothing more than a fort of upright stakes was ever built by the French at Dauphin Island, although rough stone, faced with brick, was used in the construction of the massive bastions of Fort Condé at Mobile when that fort, first built of palisades in 1711, was rebuilt in masonry in the 1720s and 1730s.

The Spaniards, however, had made use of masonry in the building of the Castillo de San Marcos in St. Augustine, between 1672 and 1695, said to be the oldest masonry fort in existence in the United States.[6] The material employed here was coquina, a native shell-rock. The design was typical of the military architecture of the period, a symmetrical structure of four bastions. It was the type perfected by Louis XIV's great military engineer, Sebastien Le Pretre,

4. Paris, Archives Nationales C–13A II, 468; hereafter PAN.
5. PAN, C–13A III, 687.
6. *Columbia Encyclopedia*, p. 1731.

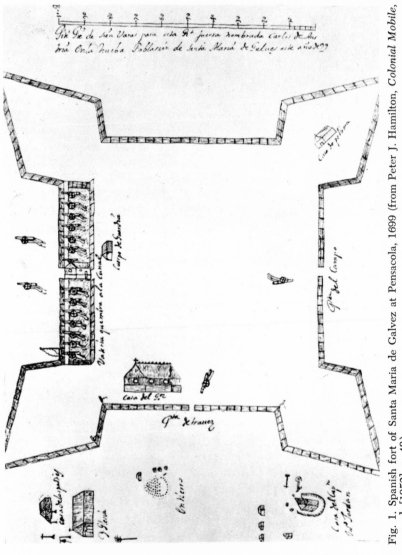

Fig. 1. Spanish fort of Santa Maria de Galvez at Pensacola, 1699 (from Peter J. Hamilton, *Colonial Mobile*, rev. ed. [1952], p. 48).

Marechal de Vauban (1633–1707), and was followed in most of the European colonies in America.

The first fort built by the Spaniards at Pensacola followed this general form, a square fort of four bastions, but like the first French forts at Biloxi and Mobile, it was of palisades, heavy timbers set upright in the ground. According to an early Spanish plan of this fort (fig. 1),[7] the bastions and curtains were of squared timbers with a platform between the seaward bastions on which about fourteen cannons were mounted. Within the fort were only a powder magazine in one of the other bastions, a small corps de garde, and a house for the governor. This was a comparatively large, apparently gable-ended structure, surmounted by a cross, indicating the presence of a chapel. Another similar structure outside the fort is marked "church" and near it a "house for the priests," with a bell and a large cross erected nearby. A house for the captain and a few cabins are the only other structures shown on this interesting document.

This fort was captured by the French on May 22, 1719, retaken by the Spanish in August, then taken again by the French on September 17, 1719.[8] From observations made by Bienville's brother de Serigny at that time, a chart of the bay and a plan of the fort were drawn up (fig. 2).[9] The fort faced southward to the entrance channel of the bay, directly opposite and north of the western tip of Santa Rosa Island on which another small fort is indicated. The platform on which the cannons were shown on the earlier plan does not appear on this later one. Instead the space is occupied by barracks and the director's lodging. Outside the curtain, between the bastions, is a large garden for the director, indicating that an attack from the sea was not anticipated. Numerous other structures are shown within the fort, including a large chapel, a new corps de garde, warehouses, and an oven.

The Jesuit Father Antoine Laval, in his *Voyage de la Louisiane*, published in 1728, quoted M. de Vienne, captain of one of the French vessels at the capture of Pensacola: "The fort of Pensacola is situated on a height of sand that commands the entrance of the harbor. . . . It is built of round logs planted as upright pickets to defend it only against the savages. There are 24 pieces of canon on

7. Peter J. Hamilton, *Colonial Mobile* (New York, 1910), p. 48.
8. P. Laval, *Voyage de la Louisiane* (Paris, 1728), p. 103.
9. Paris, Archives Nationales, Section Outremer, No. 85; hereafter PANO.

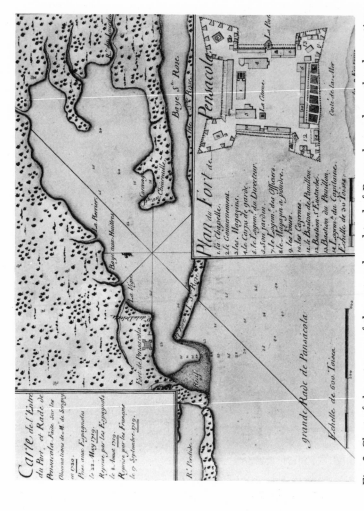

Fig. 2. Chart of the entrance of the port and roadstead of Pensacola, made on the observations of M. de Serigny in 1720; insert, plan of Fort Pensacola (PANO, 85).

four bastions, but they are very ill-mounted. . . ." He also said that, in anticipation of the French attack on Pensacola, the Spaniards had "cut down a great number of trees in order to construct a fort of stakes on the point of Santa Rosa Island: it was done in twelve days time: they made our soldier and sailor prisoners work on it." In spite of the Spanish efforts, the French took both forts and destroyed them. On their return, the Spaniards rebuilt the fort at the site of the present city of Pensacola.

The directors of the Company of the Indies in France, hoping to establish its forts and buildings in Louisiana on as permanent a basis as possible, began to concern themselves with the problems of obtaining masonry materials in the colony. On April 14, 1718, the company appointed a Monsieur Perrier as first engineer-in-chief of Louisiana. He was instructed that, after landing at Dauphin Island, he should make a study of Mobile Bay as far up as Fort Louis. His instructions also stated, "In visiting the east coast of the bay, the said sieur Perrier could see about the spot at Fish River from where one is supposed to be able to draw the stone for the fortification of Dauphin Island. He shall examine what the nature of this stone is, if it is difficult to get out and to load and at how much per cubic fathom it might come to, delivered either at Dauphin Island or at Fort Louis of Mobile, calculating the expense of a large boat and its crew. . . . He shall likewise examine what sort of oyster shell mounds there are that are said to be near Dauphin Island and which could be used for making lime. . . ."[10]

Besides looking into the availability of stone and lime, Perrier was also told to investigate the timber situation: "While the said sieur Perrier will be at Fort Louis of Mobile, he shall go to visit the saw mill that the sieur Mean has constructed on a stream which is a league away. He shall examine if it is well established, how much it could saw of planks or other wood in 24 hours, how many men are needed to serve it, and if these same men could not, in certain times, work at some cultivation or other works."

Perrier was to make use of the services of the Engineer Bajot who had been sent to build the Dauphin Island fortifications. The company's instructions were, "For the execution of these sorts of works, he could charge the sieur Bajot, captain, who was sent four years ago as engineer and is very capable of conducting building

10. Margry, *Decouvertes et etablissements,* 5:599–603.

operations because that is with which he has always been occupied."

He was also told to do what was necessary at Fort Louis of Mobile and at Dauphin Island, and to decide if the site selected for New Orleans was the proper one. Perrier never had the opportunity of carrying out these assignments; he died at Havana en route to Louisiana.[11] To avoid a recurrence of the problems caused by this event, the company appointed four engineers with Pierre LeBlond de la Tour as engineer-in-chief; the others were the Chevalier de Boispinel, Adrien de Pauger, and Charles Franquet de Chaville. By the instructions issued to them on November 8, 1719, the ship on which they were to sail was to anchor first at Pensacola which had been taken by the French that same year. They were to examine the port and draw up a plan of it, then to "think seriously about the fortification of the port of Pensacola. The Company has already given orders for the disposition of part of the materials necessary for this purpose, such as framing wood, timbers and others. . . . When the fortifications of the port of Pensacola shall have been begun, as they will not require the presence of all the engineers . . . the Sieur LeBlond de la Tour alone could suffice to conduct the works . . . [and] will make his ordinary headquarters at Pensacola. . . . He shall put it in security by the fortifications that he must have constructed there on arriving. . . ."[12]

The engineers were also to recruit workmen in France to labor on the colonial fortifications. They were to sign contracts "to serve the Company during three consecutive years at the agreed wages, which must be mediocre while the Company engages itself to feed them at the ordinary ration and to maintain them properly. The three years of their service must begin to run, for their wages from the day of engagement and for the time of service from that of their arrival in Louisiana." The workmen required by the company were listed as:

Masons, dressers, and cutters of stone
Carpenters
Locksmiths, blacksmiths, and edge tool makers
Long sawyers

11. Marc de Villiers, *Histoire de la fondation de la Nouvelle Orleans* (Paris, 1917), p. 34.
12. Margry, *Decouvertes et etablissements,* 5:610.

Brickmakers, tile makers, and lime burners
Tile floor layers
Turfers and excavators
Woodcutters and wheelwrights[13]

Persons of these trades and skills were recruited and accompanied the engineers to Louisiana.[14] Many of them died en route and more soon after they arrived, but enough survived to carry on the work, and their arrival may mark the real beginning of architectural development on the Gulf coast and in West Florida. LeBlond de la Tour, who had served in France and Spain under the Marquis d'Asfeld, the successor of Vauban as Director General of Fortifications of France, was also appointed the director of the d'Asfeld-LeBlanc Concessions in Louisiana.[15] Ignace François Broutin was in charge of the troops of these extensive concessions; he eventually succeeded de la Tour and Pauger as King's Engineer, becoming the most important architect of the French colonial period in Louisiana.[16] In 1745 he designed the most notable if not the only surviving building of that period, the second Ursuline Convent in New Orleans.[17] Also arriving in the colony in 1720, as de la Tour's draftsman, was Bernard Deverges. Upon Broutin's death in 1751, Deverges became engineer-in-chief of Louisiana, serving until his death in 1766,[18] as the colony passed from the control of France to that of Spain and England. Thus these military engineers, who all arrived in 1720, shaped the architectural development of the colony for as long as it remained under French jurisdiction, and buildings designed by them appeared not only in New Orleans but in almost every French settlement in the colony.

Among the first projects of LeBlond de la Tour in Louisiana were several plans for a fort and town at New Biloxi with a military hos-

13. PAN, B 42 bis., 312–13.
14. PAN, C–13A VI, 158.
15. Louisiana State Museum, "Records of the Superior Council," October 22, 1723.
16. Samuel Wilson, Jr., *Ignace François Broutin*, in John Francis McDermott, ed., *Frenchmen and French Ways in the Mississippi Valley* (Urbana, Ill., 1969), pp. 231–94.
17. Samuel Wilson, Jr., "An Architectural History of the Royal Hospital and the Ursuline Convent of New Orleans," *Louisiana Historical Quarterly* 29 (July 1946):559–659; hereafter *LHQ*.
18. George C. H. Kernion, "Reminiscences of the Chevalier Bernard de Verges, an Early Colonial Engineer of Louisiana," *LHQ* 7 (January 1924):56–86.

pital to be built adjacent to it.[19] These designs were all based on current French military engineering principles but were never executed because of the transfer of the capital to the newly founded city of New Orleans. At the site of the proposed new fort, camps were set up by the directors of the various concessions arriving from France (fig. 3). No doubt the plan of the d'Asfeld-LeBlanc concession was laid out by Broutin; it appears on a contemporary plan in the Paris archives.[20] The elaborate view of the Law concession camp drawn by Jean Baptiste Michel Le Bouteux, now in Chicago's Newberry Library, is one of the most extraordinary documents illustrating the early construction practices of these colonists (fig. 4). It shows elaborate tents and simple tentlike palmetto covered structures, no doubt based on Indian precedent. The large warehouse in the background is of colombage or timber frame construction built on sills laid directly on the ground, the spaces between the vertical wall timbers apparently filled in with vertical planks. The high-hipped, shingle roof pierced by several small dormer windows gives the structure an unmistakable French character. The sketch also shows men working to construct shallow-draft boats to transfer the concession to its ultimate location on the Mississippi and other men squaring construction timbers with a sort of pit saw arrangement.

Another interesting drawing of this early French period, made by the architect Alexandre DeBatz in 1732, presents the more architectural elevations of a temple and chief's cabin from a Colapissa village near New Orleans.[21] The form of these structures certainly suggests an ethnic connection between the Gulf coast natives and the Mayas of Yucatan and Central America. It was from these Indian structures that the French adapted the use of *bouzillage*, a mixture of mud and moss used in place of brick to fill in the wall spaces between the timbers of colombage frames, a material that continued to be used in Louisiana until after the mid-nineteenth century.

Numerous drawings of the buildings designed by French military engineers to be constructed at Mobile have survived in Paris archives. Many of these are plans for Fort Condé, the strongest French

19. PAN, C–13A–6, 121–24, January 8, 1721, LeBlond de la Tour to the Company of the Indies.

20. Paris, Service Hydrographique de la Marine, Atlas 4044–C f. 58.

21. Illustrated in Samuel Wilson, Jr., "Louisiana Drawings by Alexander DeBatz," *Journal of the Society of Architectural Historians* 22 (May 1963):84.

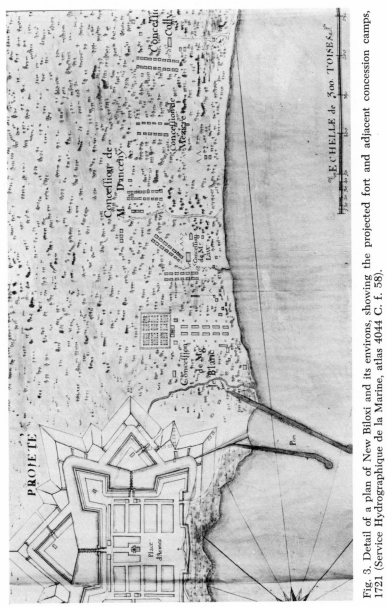

Fig. 3. Detail of a plan of New Biloxi and its environs, showing the projected fort and adjacent concession camps, 1721 (Service Hydrographique de la Marine, atlas 4044 C. f. 58).

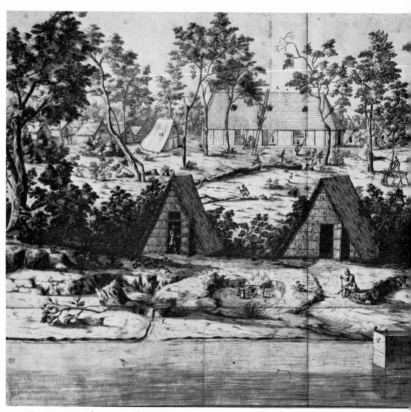

Fig. 4. Warehouse and other structures; detail from a "View of the Camp of the Concession of Monseigneur Law at New Biloxi, coast of Louisiana, drawn

by Jean Baptiste Michel Le Bouteux, 10 December, 1720" (Newberry Library).
See also endleaves.

fortification on the Gulf coast (fig. 5). Some of these plans also show elevations of the buildings proposed to be erected within the fort, notably the mansard-roofed barracks and officers' quarters that appear on several of Pauger's drawings in 1724–26 (fig. 6). These buildings were all to be of colombage construction and were almost identical to buildings proposed to be built by the Spaniards at Pensacola nearly three-quarters of a century later.

A small warehouse building designed by Pauger for Fort Condé in 1724 (fig. 7) is of particular interest because the contract and specifications as well as the architect's drawings for it exist in Paris archives. The contract document is entitled "Specifications and conditions to which will be obligated one named Fievre, master carpenter at Mobile, who presented himself in order to construct the timber-work of a projected ware-house of fifty feet of length and twenty feet of width in the clear, to be built in the fort according to the plan which had been agreed upon for it by the late M. de la Tour."[22] The specifications give interesting details of the methods employed in colombage construction, stating that "all the posts, as well as the diagonals and St. Andrew's crosses, will be connected with tenons and mortices into the sills and wall plates, erected plumb on the same alignement [sic], observing however, to give a little batter towards the top. The lintles [sic] and sills of the said doors and windows will likewise be connected with tenons and mortices into the uprights or posts which will be similarly connected into the wall plates and sills." The construction of the mansard roof is similarly described. No mention is made of the roof or wall sheathing as this contract was only for the timber framing.

The drawing shows a simple rectangular building with a single, centered entrance doorway flanked by two windows on each side and two at each end. All these openings are shown with segmental arched heads, the curve cut out of the timber lintel in exactly the same manner as found in such existing buildings as Madam John's Legacy built in 1788 in New Orleans. There were probably no glazed window sashes, the openings being closed with heavy batten shutters. The mansard roof had three curved head dormers on its front slope and was the roof form preferred for warehouses because of the added storage space it afforded. Most other roofs of the colonial period were hipped.

22. PAN, C–13A VIII, 36, April 8, 1724.

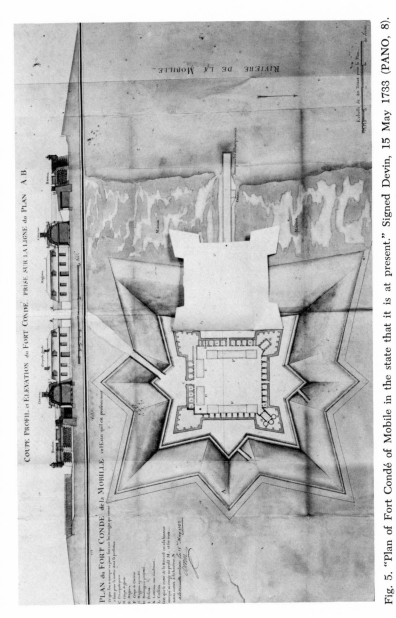

Fig. 5. "Plan of Fort Condé of Mobile in the state that it is at present." Signed Devin, 15 May 1733 (PANO, 8).

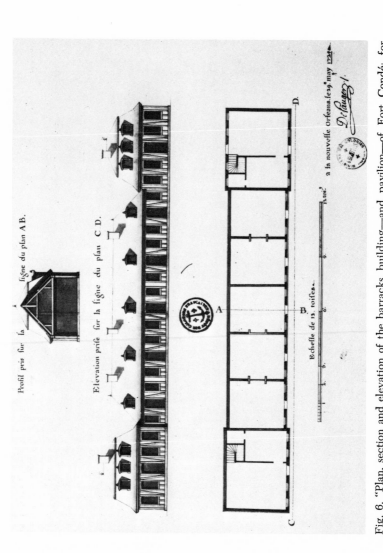

Fig. 6. "Plan, section and elevation of the barracks building—and pavilion—of Fort Condé; for lodging the officers, employees and soldiers of the garrison." Signed De Pauger, 29 May 1724 (PANO, 122).

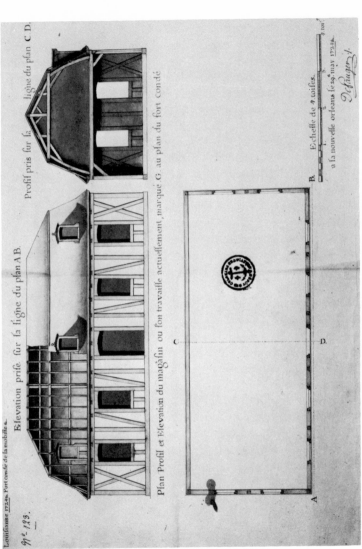

Fig. 7. "Plan, section and elevation of the warehouse on which they are actually working . . . at Fort Condé." Signed De Pauger, 29 May 1724 (PANO, 123).

Like buildings of colombage construction elsewhere in the colony, the frame buildings at Fort Condé soon deteriorated, and in April 1739 the engineer Deverges submitted a "Plan, elevation and section for two barracks projected to be built of brick masonry at Fort Condé of Mobile, in place of those that are falling in rottenness" (fig. 8). These proposed two-story structures, with masonry quoins emphasizing the corners and entrances, were quite similar in character to those that had then just been completed flanking the Place d'Armes in New Orleans. Such heavy masonry structures were found not to be the answer to construction problems in Louisiana, for with the exception of the Ursuline Convent of 1745, all such buildings failed because of foundation problems and dampness in the walls. Deverges' impressive barracks for Fort Condé were probably never constructed.

On April 1, 1751, Broutin, just a few months before his death, submitted a "Plan of the buildings projected to be built at Mobile on a large site belonging to the king, commonly called *le terrain de la Direction.*" These were three hipped-roof, one-story brick buildings arranged around three sides of a square, the front and the two rear corners of which were enclosed with fences of stakes in the ground. These new barracks were handsome structures somewhat similar to the military hospital that Broutin had built in New Orleans in 1734 next to the first Ursuline Convent. By 1751 the French engineers had reached the conclusion that brick buildings in this area should not be built more than one story high and that, where a second story was required, it should be constructed of light-weight brick between posts. Ironically, the second Ursuline Convent with solid brick walls was the only one of their structures to survive to the present time.

After Broutin's death, additional drawings were made by Alexandre DeBatz of these Mobile barracks as built, with gables rather than hipped roofs. The soldiers' barracks were described as "120 feet in length by 23 feet 4 inches in width, over all . . . constructed in masonry of stone and brick, on the site and land of the Direction, belonging to the King, which is opposite the principal entrance gate of Fort Condé of Mobile. The above dimensions, the 7 February 1752, have been taken on the grounds." The DeBatz and Broutin drawings for these barracks are now in the Archivo General de Indias in Seville. A plan, signed Phelyppeaux and dated at Mobile, November 22, 1763 (fig. 9), now in the Paris archives,

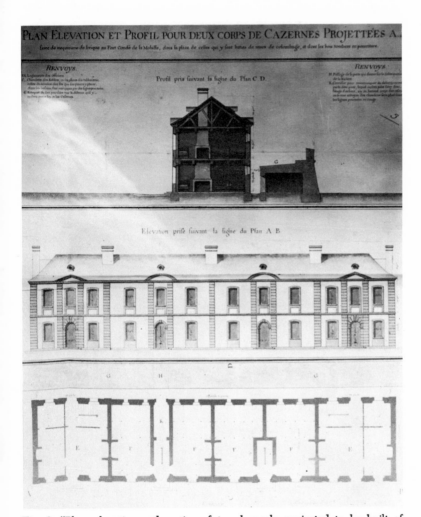

Fig. 8. "Plan, elevation and section of two barracks projected to be built of brick masonry at Fort Condé. . . ." Signed Deverges, 18 April 1739 (PANO, 3).

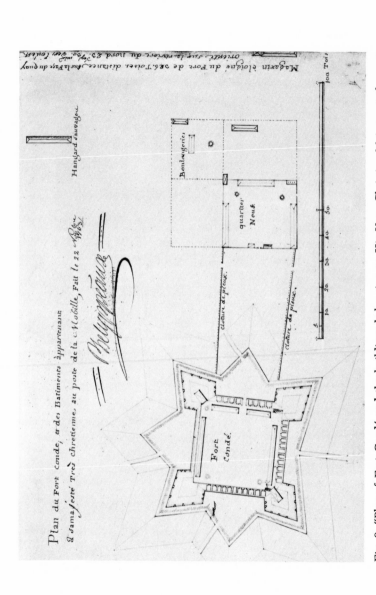

Fig. 9. "Plan of Fort Condé and the buildings belonging to His Very Christian Majesty at the post of Mobile." Signed Phelyppeaux, 22 November 1763.

shows Fort Condé as it was at the time it was transferred to England. The 1751 barracks were shown several hundred feet from the fort and connected to it by fences of stakes.

The British changed the name of Fort Condé to Fort Charlotte in honor of George III's queen, and on November 30, 1763, Major Robert Farmar submitted a report on the poor condition of the fort and its auxiliary buildings. He noted that there were barracks for 216 men within the fort "in very bad repair and wants to be rebuilt and enlarged by adding another story. . . . The officers barracks are detached from the fort about 100 yards and want a good many repairs, the floors being mostly rotten, as are many of the windows; they are sashed but mostly all the panes broke."[23] These latter barracks were the ones that had been built just ten years before.

In 1780, during the American Revolution, all of West Florida, including Mobile, Pensacola, Baton Rouge, and Natchez, was captured by the Spanish under Louisiana Governor Bernardo de Gálvez. Two years earlier Gálvez had sent Captain Jacinto Panis to Mobile. He reported that the fort was in almost ruinous condition and that the barracks were uninhabitable, having been nearly destroyed by fire, with only the walls remaining.[24] In 1793 the architect-engineer Gilberto Guillemard prepared plans for a proposed barracks building at Fort Charlotte of Mobile (fig. 10), plans so similar to the DeBatz plan of 1752 in the arrangement of doors, windows, and fireplaces as to suggest the probability that the walls of the old barracks were reused with a new, low, pitched tile roof and decorative quoins at each end in the manner of Broutin's earlier French buildings. Thus the French influence is seen to persist here throughout the colonial period. Further evidence of this is apparent in the series of sketches of old Mobile houses made in 1887 by Roderick D. McKenzie.

Even less remains of the early architecture of Pensacola. When the British took possession, Major Will. Forbes reported to the secretary of state in 1764 that "The place which is called the Fort consists of about half a mile of ground in circumference, surrounded with a rotten stockade without a ditch, so defenceless that any one

23. Dunbar Rowland, *Mississippi Provincial Archives* (Nashville, 1911), English Dominion, 1:19; hereafter *MPA*.

24. H. Mortimer Favrot, "Colonial Forts of Louisiana," *LHQ* 26 (July 1943):744.

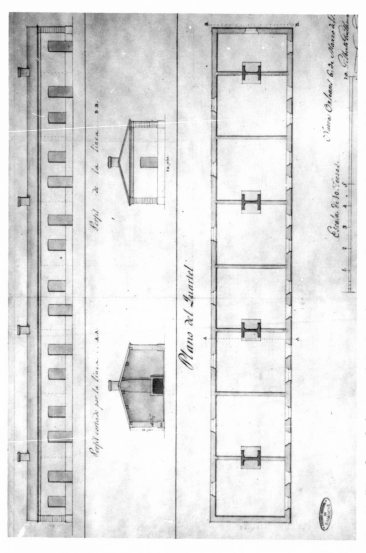

Fig. 10. "Facade and elevation of the barracks projected in Fort Charlotte of Mobile." Signed Gilberto Guillemard, March 6, 1793 (Archivo General de Simancas).

can step in at pleasure. The barracks of the officers and soldiers are nothing more than miserable bark huts, without any sort of fire places or windows, void of every necessary utencil [sic]. I enclose to your Lordship a plan of the Fort which appears fifty times better upon paper than it really is."[25]

The interesting plan (fig. 11) shows new fortifications with corner bastions "begun by Major Forbes but not finished." Within the enclosure were the governor's house with extensive gardens behind it, barracks arranged around a large parade ground, hospital, arsenal, and the other usual buildings of a fortified post. This fort was located in what is now the historic district of Pensacola, the area around Seville Square. In this area are Pensacola's oldest houses, including the Barkley House which may have been built in the 1830s on the foundations and perhaps some of the walls of a house of the 1770s. The Lavalle house, recently restored by the Pensacola Historical Restoration and Preservation Commission (now Historic Pensacola Preservation Board), and other houses of similar form that have come to be known as "French Creole" cottage— having a gallery across the front over which the slope of the gable-ended roof extends—are probably typical of the earlier houses of Pensacola and suggest an influence from the French in Mobile and New Orleans.

In 1787 the architect-engineer Guillemard prepared elaborate plans for the construction of a new fort on the site of the old Spanish fort of 1698, Fort San Carlos and Battery San Antonio, an elaborate masonry fortification in the Vauban manner (fig. 12). The buildings he proposed for construction within the fort were of colombage construction on brick piers, with mansard roofs and dormer windows, almost identical to Pauger's designs for the barracks at Mobile's Fort Condé in 1724. Little change had occurred in architectural style here in over half a century.

One of the most interesting and perhaps one of the earliest surviving structures on the Gulf coast is the so-called Krebs House or Old Spanish Fort at Pascagoula. This is a house built with a typical colombage or heavy timber frame, but here the filling between the wall timbers is a form of shell concrete, used in the earliest houses at Mobile, rather than the usual brick or mud and moss (bouzillage). Parts of this old house are believed to be one of the buildings of the De la Pointe concession established at Pascagoula in the

25. Rowland, MPA, English Dominion, 1:141.

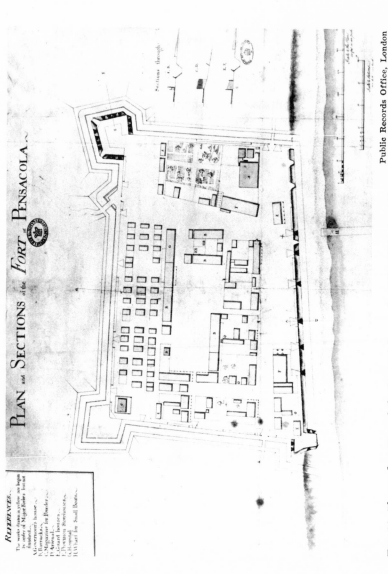

Fig. 11. Plan and section of the Fort of Pensacola, 1764 (MPA I, 141), courtesy of the Pensacola Historical Museum.

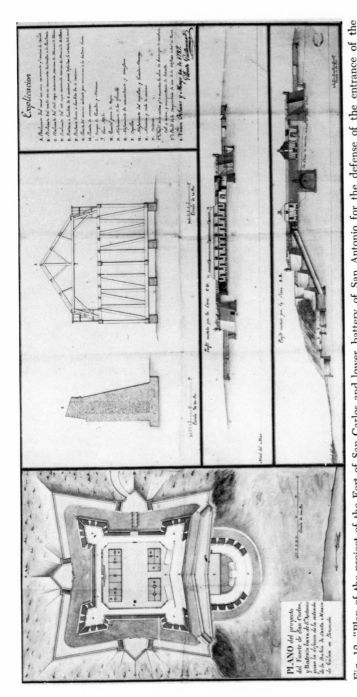

Fig. 12. "Plan of the project of the Fort of San Carlos and lower battery of San Antonio for the defense of the entrance of the Bay of Santa Maria de Galvez of Pensacola." Signed Gilberto Guillemard, May 1787 (Seville, Archivo General de Indias).

1720s, but it is not readily identifiable in Dumont De Montigny's map and sketch of this concession, made around 1730.[26] It is unlikely that one of these very early structures could have survived, but the form and construction of the Krebs house definitely link it with the buildings of the early French settlement of West Florida.

The early architecture of New Orleans is perhaps the best documented of any American city of comparable age, through plans and drawings that have been preserved in Paris archives. These were all prepared by military engineers and all reflect the influence of Vauban and his ideas of military architecture and fortification design. The city plan, designed by Pierre LeBlond de la Tour and laid out on the site in 1721 by Adrien de Pauger, is typical of the French fortified town of the period. The streets are laid out in a regular gridiron pattern with a parade ground or Place d'Armes in the center.[27] The early plans of New Orleans show enclosing fortification walls, but these were not built until after the fall of Quebec to the English, when Deverges built a palisade fortification somewhat different in design from the one originally proposed by his mentor, LeBlond de la Tour.

The first buildings were all of timber frame colombage construction covered on the outside with wide horizontal boards. These included "la Direction,"[28] the large house for the directors of the Company of the Indies to which galleries and two-story end pavillions were later added, barracks for the company's workmen and soldiers, and a windmill for which complete specifications exist and which appears in the remarkable perspective of New Orleans drawn by Jean Pierre Lassus in 1726.[29] The first building known to have been built with a brick foundation and brick between the timbers of its colombage frame was the parish church of St. Louis,[30] designed by Pauger in 1724 and dedicated at Christmas 1727. It is remarkably similar in design to Vauban's chapel in the citadel at Besancon, France. The timbers and brickwork of these "bricks between posts" buildings were always protected by wood siding or a coating of cement plaster, except for a brief period around 1730

26. Wilson, *Bienville's New Orleans*, p. 21.
27. Illustrated in Samuel Wilson, Jr., *The Vieux Carré, New Orleans, Its Plan, Its Growth, Its Architecture* (New Orleans, 1968), pp. 5–33.
28. PANO, No. 67, illustrated in Wilson, *Bienville's New Orleans*, pp. 17–18.
29. PANO, No. 71, illustrated in Wilson, *The Vieux Carré*, p. 20, and *Bienville's New Orleans*, p. 22.
30. PANO, No. 70, illustrated in Wilson, *Bienville's New Orleans*, p. 20.

when Pierre Baron served as engineer-of-the-King. He evidently liked the picturesque appearance of the exposed timber frames and left them that way in the house he designed for himself in 1730,[31] in the large building for the first Ursuline Convent, [32] and in various other structures built under his direction. This was impractical in the humid New Orleans climate, for the timbers soon rotted and the bricks deteriorated.

There followed a period of construction of large two-story brick buildings which Baron's successor, Ignace François Broutin, preferred. Thus he built the impressive barracks on the two sides of the Place d'Armes in the 1730s[33] and the second Ursuline Convent in 1745.[34] By the 1750s the barracks had collapsed because of faulty foundations and dampness in the walls. The Ursuline Convent has survived and gives an excellent idea of the impressive and monumental architectural style that appeared in the early years of French colonial Louisiana, a style originating in France and adapted by local architect-engineers from the Vauban-inspired publications on fortifications and civil and military architecture.

In more remote outposts of the French colony, buildings of a simpler type were constructed, such as the interesting colombage structures designed for Fort Tombecbé in Alabama by Bernard Deverges in 1751–59 (fig. 13). At the Balise at the mouth of the Mississippi, where Deverges served for many years, he also constructed in 1734 a small corps de garde with a hipped roof and with a gallery on two sides (fig. 14). The chapel there, not unlike the church at New Orleans, was built by Deverges from Pauger's design of about 1723.[35] Buildings of private owners on their concessions and plantations in various parts of the colony followed the same simple form as the official buildings. Dumont de Montigny depicted some of these in his crude sketches of the 1720s and 1730s, among which are the Belle Isle concessions at Natchez which show these early plantation buildings.[36]

31. PANO, Nos. 19–23, illustrated ibid., pp. 31, 32, 33.
32. PANO, No. 6, illustrated ibid., p. 38.
33. PAN, C–13A XVIII, 128, illustrated in Wilson, *Ignace François Broutin,* p. 262.
34. PANO, Nos. 10, 25, 33, illustrated in Wilson, *Bienville's New Orleans,* pp. 40, 41, 42.
35. PANO, No. 104, illustrated in Wilson, *An Architectural History,* p. 567.
36. Samuel Wilson, Jr., "Gulf Coast Architecture," in Ernest F. Dibble and Earle W. Newton, eds., *Spain and Her Rivals on the Gulf Coast* (Pensacola, 1971).

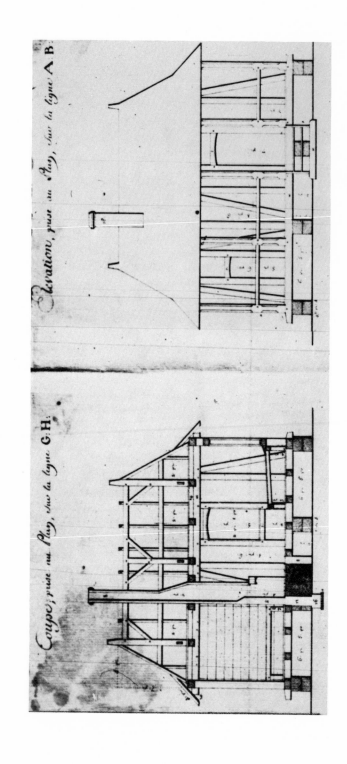

Elevation, prise au Plan, sur la ligne A.B.

Coupe, prise au Plan, sur la ligne G.H.

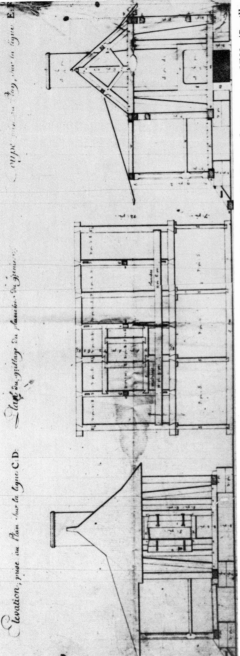

Fig. 13. Elevation and sections of the corps de garde and prison cell at Fort Tombecbé. By Bernard Deverges, 1761 (Seville, Archivo General de Indias).

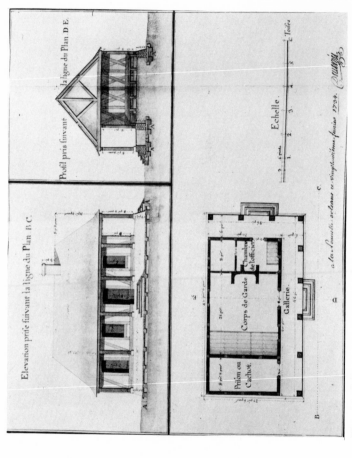

Fig. 14. "Plan, section and elevation of a corps de garde and of the prison cell projected to be built at the post of the Balize." Signed Deverges, 8 February 1734 (PANO, 224).

When Spain acquired Louisiana from France in 1763, the pilot's post at the mouth of the Mississippi, the Balise, was falling into ruin and was moved to a new site which, however, proved to be no more stable than the original. Some new buildings were erected, including a large one-story house for the commandant and officers of the garrison. This house contained ten square rooms, five on each side of a center partition. The house was surrounded by a broad gallery and had a large hipped roof. The gallery columns were simple wood posts, probably chamfered, with a balustrade of flat boards cut out in the form of classical balusters. Nearby was an open-work wood tower to serve as a lookout station from which flew the Spanish flag. These structures and their kitchens and other outbuildings are shown on an interesting but undated drawing in the Archivo General de Indias at Seville (fig. 15). A somewhat similar lookout tower still existed and was sketched by the architect B. H. Latrobe when he visited the Balise in 1819.[37]

Farther up the river at Plaquemines Bend, the French first proposed to build forts in 1747 on opposite sides of the river to defend the approaches to New Orleans.[38] These forts, St. Philip and Bourbon, were struck by a hurricane in July 1795; the west bank of the river was undermined by the action of the storm, and Fort Bourbon, a small masonry redoubt, was destroyed, collapsing into the river.[39] Plans of these two forts had been drawn up in January that year by the engineer Juan Perchet and show these two heavy masonry structures with the various buildings within them (fig. 16). In Fort Bourbon only one large barracks building existed, but Fort St. Philip contained several buildings including a large barracks, hospital, prison, warehouse, and powder magazine. Some of these were probably built by an American builder, Jacob Cowperthwait, who contracted with Spanish Governor Louis Hector de Carondelet for construction work at the Plaquemines fort in June 1792.[40] The French military engineer Vinache, who accompanied Pierre Clement Laussat to receive the colony for France from Spain in 1803,

37. Benjamin Henry Boneval Latrobe, *Impressions Respecting New Orleans,* ed. Samuel Wilson, Jr. (New York, 1951), pp. 12, 123, 166.

38. PANO, Plan of two forts at Plaquemines Bend; Nos. 56, 57, May 9, 1747.

39. Seville, Archivo General de Indias Legajo 1443B. Letter No. 738. Carondelet to Las Casas, August 30, 1795; hereafter AGI.

40. New Orleans Notarial Archives, Acts of Carlos Ximines, vol. 2, no. 310, June 20, 1792; hereafter NONA.

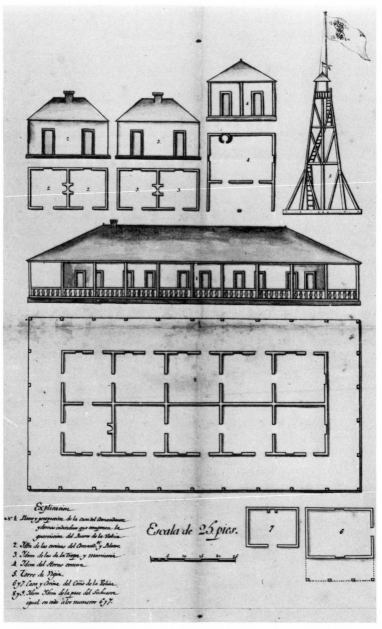

Fig. 15. Plans of the Commandant's house and various other buildings at the Balize. Unsigned, 1787.

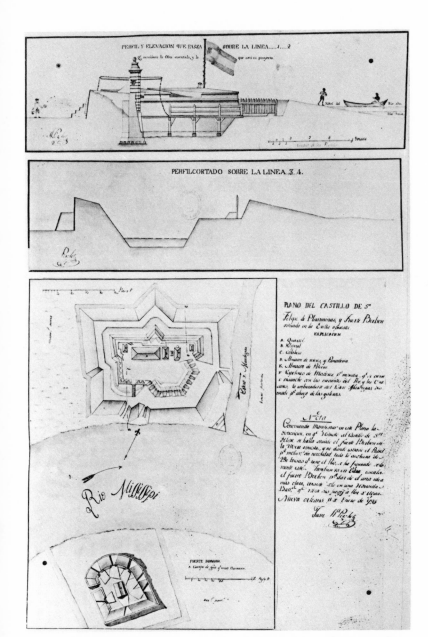

Fig. 16. "Plan of the Castillo de Sr. Filipe of Plaquemines and Fort Bourbon. . . ." Signed Juan Bta. Perchet, 10 January 1795 (Seville, Archivo General de Indias).

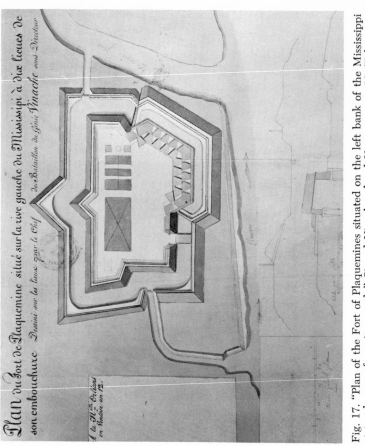

Fig. 17. "Plan of the Fort of Plaquemines situated on the left bank of the Mississippi at ten leagues from its mouth." Signed Vinache, dated Ventose, year 12 (February–March 1804) (Musée de l'Armée, Vincennes).

visited Fort St. Philip and also drew a plan of it (fig. 17), quite similar to Perchet's plan of 1795. Unfortunately neither of these plans show the appearance of the buildings within the fort. Vinache mentions in his report "Some warehouses built in bricks and covered with tiles and terraces, the whole well constructed and in the best state."[41] Other buildings of frame construction were "the large building where the commandant resides, the large barracks, the bakery . . . and . . . some houses situated outside the fort. These houses serve as hospital, as lodging to the employees, etc. all these edifices are in very good state and well built. . . ." Vinache also reported that the rebuilt Fort Bourbon was only a wooden structure, its only masonry being two chimneys.

When the French regime came to an end in 1763, many of their most important buildings in New Orleans, such as the barracks on the sides of the Place d'Armes, had already disappeared. The Deverges-designed fortifications built in 1760 were new but useless. The majority of the houses were of frame construction, raised on brick walls and piers, similar to the one now known as Madame John's Legacy. This house, though not built until 1788, followed the form and construction methods of the early French houses in the colony. This was the residence of Don Manuel Lanzos, a Spanish army captain and commandant at Mobile, whose New Orleans house was burned in the terrible Good Friday fire of 1788. Only a few days after the fire, he contracted with an American builder, Robert Jones, to build the still existing house—a Spaniard's house built by an American in the French manner.[42]

In spite of the great destruction caused by the fire of 1788 because so much wood was used in construction, the rebuilding after the fire continued in the same way, largely with brick between posts walls covered with wood siding and wood framed roofs covered with wood shingles. However, when a second conflagration devastated the city on December 8, 1794, new laws were passed requiring that roofs be covered with tiles and that the walls of brick between posts structures be protected by at least an inch of cement plaster.[43] These new laws caused considerable change in the character of the city, and tile-roofed buildings took on more of a Spanish

41. PAN, C–13A LIII, 155.
42. NONA, Acts of Pedro Pedesclaux, vol. 2, f. 427, April 1, 1788, illustrated in Wilson, *Gulf Coast Architecture*, p. 113.
43. New Orleans Public Library, Records of the Cabildo, October 9, 1795.

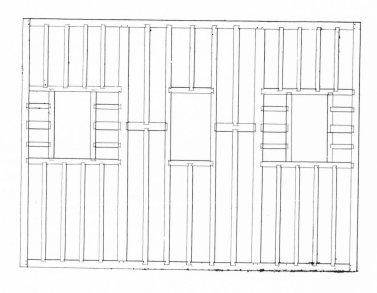

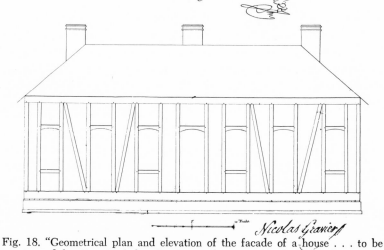

Fig. 18. "Geometrical plan and elevation of the facade of a house . . . to be constructed by Don Nicholas Gravier on lot no. 147 of the Faubourg Ste. Marie." Signed Carlos Trudeau, 23 May 1796.

flavor, such as the house built for Bartheleme Bosque, a Majorcan, in 1795 and Bernard Tremoulet's house of about 1796.[44] Both these houses, which still exist, originally had nearly flat roofs covered with square flat tiles as terraces. Houses with more steeply pitched roofs, like the Spanish school on Royal Street, used the more usual round tiles. Many of these tiles were brought from Pensacola. An advertisement in the newspaper *Moniteur de la Louisiane* for October 2, 1802, offered "Round tiles from Pensacola of the best quality that are fabricated in this country."

A few days after the 1788 fire, Carlos Laveau Trudeau, the Spanish royal surveyor, drew a plan for the subdivision of the Gravier plantation[45] adjacent to the city; it would go beyond the limits of the fortifications into what had first been part of the plantation of the city's founder, Bienville, and from 1726 until its confiscation in 1763 the plantation of the Jesuit fathers. In this new area that became known as the Faubourg St. Mary, frame construction was still permitted after the fire of 1794 and some colombage houses were built such as the one Trudeau designed for Nicolas Gravier in 1796 (fig. 18).[46] Within the area of the fortifications, however, the new buildings were mostly of all brick construction, such as the new warehouse, the new buildings around the Plaza de Armas, and the new Cabildo, Cathedral, and Presbytere all designed by Gilberto Guillemard; the Presbytere was still unfinished at the time of the Louisiana Purchase in 1803.

Many new buildings were built in the extreme western part of West Florida and other Spanish territories adjacent to it. In Baton Rouge a new fort was drawn by the engineer De Finiels in 1798,[47] and a new jail (fig. 19) the same year in Natchez, drawn by William Dunbar because there was no engineer there.[48] Also in Natchez, Connelly's Tavern and King's Tavern were built in the 1790s, both showing increasing American influences in the Spanish colony.[49] Nearby on the Natchez Trace, Mount Locust, a simple frame, one-story, gable-end house with a gallery across the front and a re-

44. Wilson, *The Vieux Carré*, p. 104, illustrated on p. 105.
45. F. P. Burns, "The Graviers and the Faubourg Ste. Marie," *LHQ* 22 (April 1939):385–427.
46. NONA, Acts of Carlos Ximines, Court Proceedings, Feb. 1801, fol. 197.
47. Madrid, Archivo Historico Militar; 7269 (Kb9–45) No. 56.
48. Archivo General de Simancas, No. 3.
49. J. Wesley Cooper, *Natchez, a Treasure of Ante-Bellum Homes* (Natchez, 1957), pp. 32–33, 144–45.

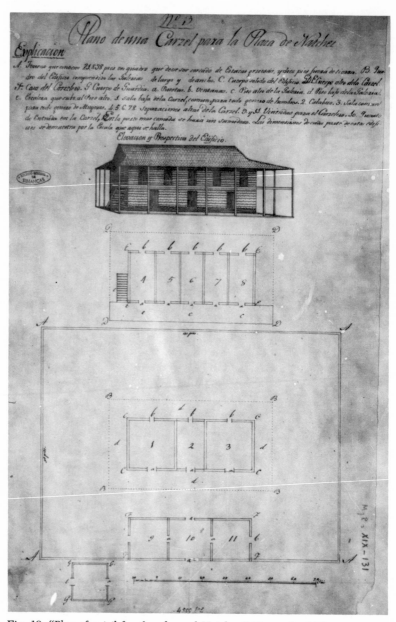

Fig. 19. "Plan of a jail for the plaza of Natchez." Drawn by William Dunbar, 1798 (Archivo General de Simancas).

cessed porch in the rear, dates also from the late eighteenth century and reflects the influence of settlers from Kentucky and Tennessee.

Along the Mississippi, between New Orleans and Baton Rouge, the American influence was less apparent in the late-eighteenth-century plantation houses. One of the finest of these, Whitehall, was probably designed by Guillemard, architect of the New Orleans Cabildo, and was in much the same style according to Christophe Colomb's early painting which records the appearance of this long-vanished mansion.[50] The Chapdu plantation in St. James Parish looked like a tiny French chateau with a two-story, square, pyramidal-roofed central element flanked by symmetrical one-story wings.[51] Homeplace, at Hahnville, built about 1790, is more typical of the earlier French style plantation house, raised on a brick basement with walls of bouzillage on the upper floor. The surrounding galleries have plastered brick columns below turned wood ones above, the great hipped roof extending over these broad galleries.[52] Homeplace has been designated by the Secretary of the Interior as a National Historic Landmark.

Few eighteenth-century buildings have survived in the Feliciana parishes above Baton Rouge. One of the most significant of these is Oakley,[53] a raised house with two stories and an attic above the basement. The louver-enclosed upper galleries are an interesting element of this fine house which also reflects the American influence in West Florida. Smaller houses such as those built along the bayous and rivers across Lake Pontchartrain from New Orleans show a little more French feeling. The early-nineteenth-century lodge at the Boy Scout Camp Salmen is not unlike the typical so-called Creole cottage of Pensacola. Thus did French, Spanish, and American influences affect the character of the architecture of eighteenth-century West Florida, and continued to influence its development through most of the succeeding century.

50. H. Parrott Bacot, *The Louisiana Landscape 1800–1969* (Baton Rouge, 1969), p. 8.
51. Historic New Orleans Collection, The Kemper and Leila Williams Foundation; Richard Koch bequest.
52. Library of Congress, Historic American Buildings Survey, La. 155.
53. J. Wesley Cooper, *A Treasure of Louisiana Plantation Homes* (Natchez, 1961), pp. 60–61.

Colonial Painting and Furniture in a Florida Borderland

JESSIE J. POESCH

IN the last fifty years there have been numerous studies and publications about the arts and crafts of colonial America—some superficial, others meticulously researched and written. Very few of these have dealt with the southernmost states, partly because it has been assumed—indeed often correctly—that comparatively little has survived from these areas. Populations were smaller; wars, fires, hurricanes, and other natural disasters seem to have been more frequent. In the Floridas, archaeological research is beginning to provide valuable fragments of evidence; careful study of documents may gradually provide further information, even if the actual objects are irretrievable.

A number of paintings done in the colonial era have been known for some time in lower Louisiana, though research will no doubt uncover more.[1] Until relatively recently it has been assumed that virtually no furniture had survived from the colonial period or from the early nineteenth century.[2] However, the efforts of a num-

---

1. The best collection of paintings done in the colonial era of Louisiana is in the Louisiana State Museum, 751 Chartres Street, New Orleans, and I am grateful to the director, Mrs. Peggy Richards, for permission to use examples from this. Publications include Isaac Monroe Cline, *Art and Artists in New Orleans during the Last Century* (New Orleans, 1922); Louisiana Library Commission, *Louisiana, A Guide to the State*, Writers Program of the Work Projects Administration, 3d printing (New York, 1945), pp. 161–77; and W. Joseph Fulton and Roulhac B. Toledano, "Portrait Painting in Colonial and Ante-bellum New Orleans," *Antiques Magazine* 93 (June 1968):788–89.

2. Charles van Ravenswaay, "The Creole Arts and Crafts of Upper Louisiana," *Bulletin of the Missouri Historical Society* (April 1956), p. 219.

ber of astute collectors and recent research have identified over eighty pieces which appear to date from those periods.[3] It is expected that additional research will gradually reveal other examples. At present only a few other artifacts from this era have been identified. More archaeological investigation and analyses of documents are still needed.

The earliest pictorial records of New Orleans are the topographical views of the city by military men trained more by draftsmen than by professional painters. From their work we can see the change in the appearance of the settlement from the small village in a swampy terrain, depicted by Jean Pierre Lassus in 1726, to the well-established town shown in a 1765 drawing, probably done by an English military man.[4]

In 1819 the architect Benjamin Henry Latrobe, who died in New Orleans in 1820, painted many watercolors while in that city. These include a view of one of the Spanish-type flat rooftops of New Orleans which also shows a man seated on a typical Mexican or Spanish sling chair.[5] Another is of the market place, in which he sketched the heterogeneous populace of the growing port city. He wrote: "The articles to be sold were not more various than the sellers. White men and women, & of all hues of brown & of all classes of faces, from round Yankees, to grisly and lean Spaniards, black negroes & negresses, filthy Indians half naked, mulattoes, curly & straight-haired, quarteroons of all shades, long-haired and frizzled, the women dressed in the most flaring yellow & scarlet gowns, the men capped & hatted. Their wares consisted of as many kinds as their faces."[6]

We know that in the late eighteenth and early nineteenth cen-

3. Jessie J. Poesch, "Early Louisiana *armoires*," *Antiques Magazine* 94 (August 1968):196–205; Poesch, *Early Furniture of Louisiana, 1750–1830* (New Orleans: Louisiana State Museum, 1972), 85 pp. The material in this paper is partly condensed from these studies.

4. The Lassus drawing is in the National Archives, Paris; the 1765 drawing is in the Louisiana State Museum.

5. Reproduced in Benjamin Henry Boneval Latrobe, *Impressions Respecting New Orleans*, ed. Samuel Wilson, Jr. (New York, 1951), facing p. 60. Thomas Jefferson called these chairs "campeachy" chairs, referring either to their place of origin in Campeche or to the wood of that name. Very similar ones are still occasionally imported into New Orleans from Mexico. For a picture of a somewhat similar form made in New York, see Charles F. Montgomery, *American Furniture, The Federal Period* (New York, 1966), cat. no. 120, pp. 165–66.

6. Latrobe, *Impressions*, p. 22.

turies a number of painters lived and worked in the city and in the surrounding area for at least short periods of time, though few, if any, appear to have made their permanent homes there. This situation is perhaps little different from most other small American cities, or from smaller European cities; there was not always enough full-time business to support an artist. These itinerant or semi-itinerant painters were chiefly portrait painters, for it was the likeness, the portrait, that people most wished to have.

The most important artist who worked in and around New Orleans in the last quarter of the eighteenth century was Joseph Salazar de Mendoza, who died in that city in 1802. He was of Spanish descent and emigrated to Louisiana from the Yucatan. Among Salazar's portraits is one of Lieutenant Miguel Dragon, which is now in the collection of the Louisiana State Museum (fig. 1). Dragon was born in Athens, Greece, and his original name was Dracos. He served in the artillery campaign of Don Bernardo de Gálvez against the English in West Florida during the American Revolution. Dragon was later commissioned a lieutenant by Charles II of Spain and was assigned to Almonester's regiment in New Orleans. He is portrayed in the portrait in a rather stiff, closed pose, in which the left arm is held akimbo and the right hand is tucked into the waistcoat. This is apparently typical of Salazar's handling. However, it is also typical of the stance and style of the period, for one finds figures of comparable rank similarly posed in the works of Goya.[7] A related painting of Lieutenant Dragon's daughter shows her with the feminine attribute of flowers (fig. 2). She married a M. Dimitry in 1799, which may be the date and occasion of the painting. Dimitry was a New Orleans merchant of Greek origin. His wife is shown seated on a Windsor chair, evidence of the kind of furniture used in this area. These were very probably imported from the East; there is no evidence to suggest that they were made in lower Louisiana.[8] Windsor chairs are seen in another painting attributed to Salazar, in which Dr. Joseph Montegut and his family are seated as if gathered together for a musical evening (fig. 3).[9]

7. Data from records of Louisiana State Museum. The figure is posed the same way in Goya's portrait of Dr. Peral, c. 1795, in the National Gallery, London.

8. Of the various references on Windsor chairs, probably the most useful is Thomas H. Ormsbee, *The Windsor Chair* (New York, 1962).

9. Data from records of Louisiana State Museum, where the picture is on loan.

Fig. 1. Joseph Salazar de Mendoza, portrait of Lt. Miguel Dragon. Collection of Louisiana State Museum, New Orleans.

Fig. 2. Joseph Salazar de Mendoza, portrait of Marianne Celeste Dragon. Collection of Louisiana State Museum, New Orleans.

Photo by Betsy Swanson

Fig. 3. Joseph Salazar de Mendoza, portrait of Dr. Joseph Montegut and family. Collection of Louisiana State Museum, New Orleans.

Fig. 4. Unknown artist, portrait of Pere Antoine de Sedella. Private collection.

Montegut was born in France in 1735 and served as a surgeon major in the Spanish army. He died in New Orleans in 1819.

Père Antoine de Sedella, a Capuchin priest from Malaga, Spain, who first came to New Orleans in 1781, was painted at least twice (fig. 4). One of these is a remarkable life-size portrait of him at the age of seventy-four, painted by Edmund Brewster in 1822. It is owned by St. Louis Cathedral in New Orleans, where Père Antoine was rector for over forty years. The venerable Père Antoine was apparently something of a benevolent tyrant, and one can almost sense this in the lean, intense face which the artist delineated. Brewster was a little-known artist who worked occasionally in New Orleans in the years between 1819 and 1824.[10] Though he also painted a large-scale copy of Stuart's Lansdowne portrait of George Washington, which still hangs in New Orleans' old City Hall, he seems to have earned his living by doing small portraits.

Though we can now point to many pieces of furniture which it is thought were made in lower Louisiana in the late eighteenth or early nineteenth century, in no single case is the documentation or history impeccable. Craftsmen do not often leave documentation. Since there were no newspapers in the area until the late eighteenth century, we lack even the kind of information gained from advertisements, lists of offerings of goods for sale, etc. However, through careful examination of pieces in eighteenth-century taste which have a reasonably firm history of having been in this region for some time, a number of common characteristics have become identifiable. Style, use of certain woods, and history in the region have been the criteria used in this kind of analysis. In certain ways the furniture believed to be from this area differs from the Anglo-American or English furniture of the same period, and also from French and Canadian furniture, although there is much overlapping.

One characteristic that emerges is a decidedly French feeling. This is logical enough—though French rule terminated in 1763–64, and was briefly reinstated in 1803, French people continued to be attracted to the area. Two important influxes of French were the

10. George G. Groce and David H. Wallace, *The New York Historical Society's Dictionary of Artists in America, 1564–1860* (New Haven, 1957), p. 79. For a rendering of Père Antoine by a more primitive artist, see Fulton and Toledano, "Portrait Painting," fig. 7, p. 791.

migrations of Acadians from Canada, who settled largely in the Bayou Teche country after the French and Indian War, and the influx of refugees after the slave uprisings in Santo Domingo in the late eighteenth and early nineteenth centuries.

Among surviving pieces, the armoire, or wardrobe, occurs most frequently. This is probably because it is such a useful and versatile storage piece. The armoire is an essentially continental form and is found throughout France, Germany, and Holland, but it is comparatively rare in the Anglo-American east coast and in England during the period under consideration.[11] At least two examples of armoires, relatively small in scale, are made of cypress, a wood native to lower Louisiana and seldom found in comparable pieces in France or Canada.[12] The wood is used generously and the panels are thick, suggesting a ready availability of material at that time.

More sophisticated pieces of mahogany have survived, sometimes combined with a different secondary wood.[13] On two of these— and on one of the cypress armoires—the edges of the upper panels are shaped in the curves and countercurves typical of Louis XV design. One can surmise either that the craftsmen were trained in Europe or that there were examples for them to see which had been brought from the Continent (fig. 5).[14] Mahogany would have been readily available from the West Indies. It is also possible that mahogany furniture found in Louisiana might have been made in the islands and brought to Louisiana by some of the more fortunate refugees. However, if little furniture of the eighteenth century has survived in Louisiana and West Florida, still less seems to have remained in the islands. One scholar who investigated the subject concluded that in the Danish West Indies "there were no good cabinet-makers capable of making furniture on the spot," and cites one traveler's description which suggests that in the islands, despite a certain affluence, furnishings were often very simple.[15] Moreover, she concluded that one eighteenth-century armoire found in the islands had probably been crafted in New Orleans.[16]

11. See Poesch, "Early Louisiana *armoires.*"
12. Poesch, *Early Furniture of Louisiana,* cat. nos. 1 and 5. For roughly comparable pieces from Canada, see Jean Palardy, *The Early Furniture of French Canada* (New York, 1965), pp. 47–144.
13. Poesch, *Early Furniture of Louisiana,* cat. nos. 3 and 4.
14. Ibid., p. 2.
15. Inge Mejer Antonsen, "Homes and Furniture in the Danish West Indies," *Dansk Kunsthåndvaerk* (1967–68), pp. 187–93; trans. David Hohnen.
16. Letter and photograph from Mrs. Antonsen, January 7, 1970.

Fig. 5. Mahogany armoire. Collection of Mr. and Mrs. James Didier.

A small group of furniture comes from the Ursuline Convent in New Orleans, established in 1727. Convent records do not indicate when or if this furniture was made for the convent or brought to the convent, but there is reason to believe that it has been continuously owned by the convent since some time in the eighteenth century. The group includes several tables of walnut, two armoires —both of walnut and cypress—and a low buffet of cypress.[17] The lines are those of high-style French Louis XV, but rather than elaborate carving or painting for decorative effect, such as would be found on comparable French pieces, the polished surfaces of the fine-grain hardwoods suffice as decoration. One of this group is the small table shown in figure 6. The scalloped skirt, the restrained but springing curve of the cabriole legs, and the discreet hoof feet are all typical.

Another unknown fact about this furniture is the identity of the cabinetmakers. We know from census data that woodworkers were listed among the earliest settlers,[18] though it is doubtful that any of the surviving furniture would have been made by these men. Later censuses do not list men by crafts. Some estate inventories list Negro slaves by crafts, and cabinetmakers are among them. On occasion one also finds surprisingly extensive lists of cabinet-making tools.[19] It is possible that some of the plantation owners made their own furniture. Dom Francisco Bouligny, an official of the Spanish government, wrote in 1776 of the Creoles: "There are few houses of which the furniture has not been made by the owners themselves, and men of means do not disdain to pass entire days handling a plane, in the carpenter shop, or the blacksmith shop."[20] We forget, perhaps, the versatility of some men of the Enlightenment.

In one case there is an inscription on the bottom of an armoire, reading "Glapion" and written in late eighteenth- or early nineteenth-century script.[21] A member of this New Orleans family is listed in Gibson's *New Orleans Guide and Directory* of 1838 as a carpenter and a free man of color. The armoire is in a style earlier

17. Poesch, *Early Furniture of Louisiana*, cat. nos. 9–12, 22.

18. "Sidelights on Louisiana History," *Louisiana Historical Quarterly* (January 1918):134–38.

19. Edith Dart Price, trans., "Inventory of the Estate of Sieur Jean Baptiste Prevost, Deceased Agent of the Company of the Indies, July 13, 1769," *Louisiana Historical Quarterly* (July 1926):411–98.

20. As quoted by Alcée Fortier, *A History of Louisiana* (Paris, 1904), 2:33.

21. Poesch, *Early Furniture of Louisiana,* cat. no. 7, see especially fig. 7a.

Fig. 6. Walnut table with saltire stretchers, from the Ursuline Convent of New Orleans, probably c. 1760–80. Collection of Dr. and Mrs. Robert Judice.

Fig. 7. Mahogany blanket chest. Collection of Hugh Allison Smith.

than that of 1838, but it is possible that an ancestor of this man fashioned it. Indeed, there is a long tradition of skilled craftsmen in this family, and until very recently there were practicing cabinet-makers in it. This is a slender bit of evidence, but it is important because it comes close to affirming the existence of working cabinet-makers in New Orleans and lower Louisiana during the late eighteenth century.

Commentary

CHARLES VAN RAVENSWAAY

THESE two papers by Mr. Wilson and Professor Poesch represent pioneering efforts in the rediscovery of information that has been ignored in the past. Such studies require research in manuscript and other source materials found in this country as well as in France, Spain, Britain, and elsewhere, and require the location and study of surviving examples of architecture and furniture made during the colonial period, or shortly afterward in the colonial tradition.

Few buildings remain along the Gulf coast from the French and Spanish colonial periods, and most of these are public or religious buildings, such as the Castillo de San Marcos in St. Augustine and the original portions of the Presbytere, the Cabildo, and the Ursuline Convent in New Orleans. Almost no domestic buildings appear to have survived. Furniture made during the colonial period is also very rare. Apparently no pieces made in Florida are known to exist. In Florida, as in Louisiana, the climate, changing fashions, and a general indifference to preserving such pieces, among other factors, have led to the destruction of most of the thousands of pieces that once existed, which were either made in Louisiana or imported from France, the West Indies, Mexico, and elsewhere. Fortunately, collectors are now seeking out and preserving the remaining examples, and although most of those available for study now are simplified versions of sophisticated designs, some are the products of skilled craftsmen who followed the fashions of the late eighteenth and early nineteenth centuries, particularly in the use of inlay. It is hoped that in time some pieces of an earlier design, particularly those using carved details, can be found. Such pieces were made in French Canada and Upper Louisiana and one can assume that they were also made in Louisiana and perhaps in West Florida. Possibly also pieces made in the Spanish design tradition will also be located, although it is not likely that many such pieces were made in Louisiana, for the colony remained predominately French in its culture during the years of Spanish domination.

As both Mr. Wilson and Dr. Poesch have suggested, the history of design in the Gulf area must be studied in relation to its political and social history as well as to the construction and making of furniture in other parts of the Spanish and French colonies in North America. Much of that history concerns the international rivalry among France, England, and Spain for control of the continent: the attempt of each of these powers to direct even minor colonial affairs from Europe, and the inevitable compromises which the overwhelming size of the continent, its climate, diseases, and natural products necessitated. The settlements included people of many races including African and Indian, each with different cultural traditions. This mélange influenced the kinds of buildings constructed and the objects used in them. We can only partially appraise these complex influences now. A more complete understanding will require the work of scholars in many fields, particularly in anthropology and archaeology. There are many questions to be answered. Did Indian and African construction techniques influence in any way local building at any period, or the design and making of objects? What were the local woods used in the construction of houses and in the making of furniture? How extensive was the commerce in lumber? We know that New Orleans before the end of the eighteenth century was being supplied with white pine from the Pittsburgh area, and that Florida pine lumber was shipped in considerable quantities from St. Augustine in the 1760s to the islands. Indeed the story of the Gulf trade during the colonial period and the American Revolution era remains to be explored, as does importation of luxury items such as furniture, metal and glasswares, fabrics, and other objects. Excavations in St. Augustine reveal fragments of Chinese as well as European ceramics. Furniture and other wares from the West Indies were commonly imported in New Orleans. Professor Poesch has indicated that evidence is still lacking to differentiate between furniture based upon French designs made in the West Indies and that made in Louisiana.

In the Gulf coast settlements, as in the settlements on all frontiers, the contrast between elegant and primitive was constantly present. Society was fluid; there was a quality of impermanence about many of the settlements which made difficult the orderly development of political, economic, social, and cultural patterns. This was not the case in the British colonial towns like Charleston, Savannah, and St. Augustine, along the Atlantic coast. The short lives of some Gulf settlements, the fires, floods, attacks from enemies, and diseases that many of these communities suffered, gave uncertainty to individual lives and efforts and disrupted orderly communal growth. Not until the close of the colonial period did life along the Gulf area acquire some political and economic stability. It was then that architecture and cabinetwork flourished in the designs, building techniques, and use of materials required by the climate and the sites. Despite the political differences during the early years of settlement, many of the colonists and their descendants survived largely because the French and the Spanish did not try to possess the land and to make warfare against the Indians so much a way of life as had the British. Instead, they came in search of furs and souls which the Indians conveniently possessed. To garner both they sought to live at peace with their Indian allies and succeeded remarkably well.

Both of our speakers have indicated the importance of the French and Spanish archives in their continuing studies. These have survived in great numbers but have yet to be systematically examined. We are much indebted to a number of remarkable historians, many of them nonprofessional, for their local and regional histories. The complete story of the French and Spanish regimes in North America is not likely to be written until the colonial archives are collected, translated, edited, and published. Professor Poesch and Mr. Wilson have shown us what rich material is to be found about buildings and furniture, but they have been able to make only a sampling. I can think of no more important opportunity for our American Revolution Bicentennial than to make those archives available for scholars everywhere.

The recognition by the Florida Bicentennial Commission and the University of Florida of the importance of such studies in our colonial past is a hopeful sign. This recognition is given further strength by the invitation extended to Professor Poesch and Mr. Wilson to discuss the visual arts, a subject often overlooked at scholarly conferences such as this symposium. Professor Poesch and Mr. Wilson have been very generous with their knowledge. Their careful research and the limited time in which they had to present their subjects merit our admiration and appreciation.